Democracy and Community

T0056405

Democracy and Community

Jean-Luc Nancy
Peter Engelmann

Translated by Wieland Hoban

polity

First published in German as *Demokratie und Gemeinschaft* © 2015 Passagen Verlag, Ges. M.b.H, Vienna. English language edition published by arrangement with Eulama Lit. Ag.

This English edition © Polity Press, 2019

Author photo on p.vi © Passagen Verlag

Polity Press
65 Bridge Street
Cambridge CB2 1UR, UK

Polity Press
101 Station Landing
Suite 300
Medford, MA 02155, USA

ISBN-13: 978-1-5095-3534-7 (hardback)
ISBN-13: 978-1-5095-3535-4 (paperback)

A catalogue record for this book is available from the British Library.

Typeset in 12.5 on 15pt Adobe Garamond
by Fakenham Prepress Solutions, Fakenham, Norfolk NR21 8NL
Printed and bound in Great Britain by CPI Group (UK) Ltd, Croydon

The publisher has used its best endeavours to ensure that the URLs for external websites referred to in this book are correct and active at the time of going to press. However, the publisher has no responsibility for the websites and can make no guarantee that a site will remain live or that the content is or will remain appropriate.

Every effort has been made to trace all copyright holders, but if any have been overlooked the publisher will be pleased to include any necessary credits in any subsequent reprint or edition.

For further information on Polity, visit our website:
politybooks.com

Contents

I

Rethinking the Political

Peter Engelmann: I'd like to start our conversation with your biography. I'd like to trace the development of your thought and your philosophical positions by looking at your intellectual career. What concrete historical experiences have played a part here, what are your central philosophical reference points? So, you moved to Paris to study philosophy there ...

Jean-Luc Nancy: Yes, I came to Paris in 1959 and studied at the Sorbonne from 1960 to 1964.

Peter Engelmann: You wrote your thesis under Ricœur's supervision, and then you became his assistant. What significance did Ricœur have for you?

Jean-Luc Nancy: No, no, Ricœur was my doctoral supervisor but I was never his assistant; things didn't turn out like that. In 1964 I passed the *agrégation*, which was the entrance examination for prospective teachers, and, because back then one could choose the city where one wanted to teach, I chose Strasbourg, as I wanted to study theology too. Strasbourg is the only place in France where the public university has a theology department. This is connected with the fact that Alsace-Lorraine didn't belong to France in 1905, when the strict separation of church and state was implemented there. The concordat of 1801 applies to this day in Alsace. At any rate, I didn't get a position in Strasbourg, but I did find a very good one in Colmar, and so I started teaching in Colmar in the autumn of 1964 and studied theology in Strasbourg at the same time. But I realized very soon that the theology course was very weak and completely uninteresting, so I soon abandoned it. But I had made connections at the university, and one day I was asked if I'd be interested in giving lectures on structuralism.

Structuralism was considered *the* new thing, but people didn't know anything about it outside Paris. In addition to that, I also did a seminar on Hegel. And there was actually no one at the university in Strasbourg at the time who was familiar with Hegel, so they asked me, as I'd already occupied myself quite intensively with Hegel's philosophy; it had also been one of the subjects for the *agrégation* examination.

Peter Engelmann: So, in terms of your intellectual context, you would have belonged more in Paris than in Strasbourg. What factors led you to stay there?

Jean-Luc Nancy: Well, first of all, as I said, I wanted to study theology; then there were the courses offered at the university; and finally, of course, meeting Philippe Lacoue-Labarthe also played a part. He came to Strasbourg in 1967, we got acquainted through Lucien Braun. Braun had the idea that one should bring Philippe and me together, that something could come about from that. And he was right! As it turned out there were many shared affinities, such as Heidegger, but most of all Derrida. And situationism. In the mid-sixties Strasbourg was the city of the situationists; not the core circle around Guy Debord, but many had come to Strasbourg to attend Henri Lefebvre's lectures; his critique of bourgeois society was very popular at the time. In 1966 they wrote a little pamphlet, *On the Poverty of Student Life*,[1] which was very well written, in the style of Debord, and handed it out at the official opening of the semester, a ceremony attended by all the professors. There was a scandal! But I didn't actually witness it directly, as I was doing my military service at the time.

Peter Engelmann: How long did you have to serve in the army?

Jean-Luc Nancy: Just for a year; I taught at the military school in Strasbourg. That was where people went to do their A-levels, or, if they were already in the army, to attend the military academy in Saint-Cyr directly afterwards. Normally the academy only admits candidates who have attended preparatory classes at university, but one can also work one's way up from the army. I was teaching philosophy to the A-level students and cultural subjects to the officer cadets.

Peter Engelmann: I don't think there's any such emphasis on a comprehensive cultural education at higher military schools in Germany or Austria.

Jean-Luc Nancy: Well, in France one expects a certain level of culture, at least from the higher-ranking officers. Certainly, they all had to take A-levels, and philosophy was one of the subjects. Naturally, teaching philosophy at a military school was a slightly peculiar affair. One time I had selected a text by Marx for an examination, and the captain had to be informed of the exam topics in advance. I was promptly summoned by the colonel, who said, 'Nancy, I can't allow that. A text by Marx at a military school!' I replied, 'But Colonel, read the text, it's an analysis of society!' to which he answered, 'Nonetheless, it's impossible.' Another time, *Esprit* wanted to arrange a discussion between Althusser and me after I published an article about Althusser in that journal. So, I needed permission to travel to Paris for two days. But the colonel said at the time, 'You see, a discussion with Althusser, a member of the communist party, I can't allow that.'

Peter Engelmann: Not even a discussion!

Jean-Luc Nancy: A month or two later my grand-mother, the mother of my father, passed away. So I went to the colonel again. And this time I naturally received permission to go to Paris for a few days for the funeral.

Peter Engelmann: Let me recapitulate briefly: you went to Colmar in 1964 and taught there, and in 1966 you spent a year at the military school in Strasbourg.

Jean-Luc Nancy: Yes, in 1967 I taught in Colmar again and worked at the university in Strasbourg at the same time, but that was just the course on Hegel.

Peter Engelmann: And you met Philippe that same year.

Jean-Luc Nancy: Yes. Philippe had come to Strasbourg because an influential professor in Bordeaux was well disposed towards him. Georges Gusdorf had taken him along to Strasbourg. That's how it was back then. In my case, it was Ricœur who wanted me to join him in Nanterre shortly afterwards. Although I must say that I was not very close to Ricœur. I didn't really have a strong connection to anyone in Strasbourg, so Philippe and I weren't really tied to Strasbourg. But, as I said, Lucien Braun was also in Strasbourg, and we had the feeling that he was very open and that there might be a possibility of starting something new with him. So we thought about staying in Strasbourg, and I asked Ricœur if he would mind if I didn't follow him to Nanterre.

Peter Engelmann: You had to ask him for permission because he was your doctoral supervisor?

Jean-Luc Nancy: No, no, there weren't any strict regulations about that, I just felt I owed it to him. Though I didn't know at the time that Gusdorf, like Ricœur, was a rather influential personality among French Protestants. Naturally Ricœur was a far more significant philosopher, though Gusdorf wasn't actually working in the same areas as Ricœur. Only much, much later did it occur to me that maybe Gusdorf relished the fact that a student of Ricœur had come to him. That's very likely, in fact. Because he knew, of course, that I'd written my master's thesis on Hegel and religion under Ricœur's supervision, and my doctoral thesis on Kant from 1967 to 1968. In any case, it was really pure coincidence that I ended up in Strasbourg, a mixture of coincidences.

Peter Engelmann: Well, I wouldn't only call them coincidences; it came about through several factors in your life.

Jean-Luc Nancy: There was another reason for me to stay in Strasbourg: I didn't want to return to Paris because the family of my wife, whom I had met in Paris, lived there. My parents had also moved there by then, they'd gone to Paris during my studies.

Peter Engelmann: Where did your parents live before that?

Jean-Luc Nancy: In various cities; we often moved house, because my father was an engineer in the army. After the First World War, his father had said, 'I want my son to learn German, so that there won't be another war between Germany and France in the future.' Many people in France thought that way at the time, maybe in Germany too. So my father was sent to Germany, to Baden-Baden. We lived there from the mid-forties to the early fifties, so I also spoke German during that time. Then we were in Bergerac, in the Dordogne, and from there we moved to Toulouse. There I attended the preparatory classes for the École Normale, because my father wanted to send me to a Grande École, but I never went to the École Normale.

Peter Engelmann: You mentioned before that Philippe, and you too, were influenced by situationism, an artistic and intellectual movement that was very active in Strasbourg at the time.

Jean-Luc Nancy: Yes, naturally the situationists were also a factor. Without realizing it, Philippe and I had a mutual friend, Daniel Joubert; like Philippe, he came from Bordeaux. I had met him in Paris, it was around 1962. He was very close to the situationists but never had a leading function, because he was an anarchist and refused to be integrated into a prescribed order. As you know, Debord was almost a dictator of sorts. Joubert was incredibly clever and a wonderful person, and he acted as a connection between Philippe and me. Because Philippe, like me, had a great deal in common with Daniel – as well as situationism also an interest in Bonhoeffer, for example. Daniel came from a Protestant background, and Bonhoeffer was a central figure for Protestants on the left. I myself came from a Catholic background, but Protestantism was also very important for me. Jacques Ellul was also in Bordeaux during the fifties and sixties, he too was a Protestant, he lectured on the relationship between technology and society and was familiar with Heidegger. That's somewhat bizarre, Heidegger and Bonhoeffer .… These different influences created a kind of patchwork, one could say, though the central impulse was probably to conceive of society in a non-Marxist way. Because Marxism, or perhaps more the idea of revolution, was dominant at that time. So we wanted to be, or were supposed to be, revolutionary, but at the same time we knew that there was no longer a political model for a revolution.

Peter Engelmann: But hang on, we're talking about the late sixties; that was when the French left was still dominated by the Communist Party of France (PCF), and they certainly thought they knew how this revolutionary business works!

Jean-Luc Nancy: Yes, but we already sensed at the time that the communist party wouldn't keep that up. It was already clear in 1956. Budapest, the suppression of the Hungarian popular uprising, that was a great shock!

Peter Engelmann: So, you and the others were already criticizing Stalinism around 1956, and you also witnessed the de-Stalinization carried out by Khrushchev, the self-criticism of the communist party?

Jean-Luc Nancy: Yes.

Peter Engelmann: How old were you then, in 1956?

Jean-Luc Nancy: I was born in 1940. So I was 16 and still in Bergerac, Philippe was in Bordeaux.

Peter Engelmann: So you were already political at a very early age?

Jean-Luc Nancy: Yes, I was politicized, if one can call it that, through the Catholic left. Philippe was part of the Protestant left. And Algeria was a big issue for all of us. We realized that the French communist party hadn't taken Algeria's side decisively enough. That was another factor that distanced us from the party. After the war, we realized that the new Algeria wasn't quite as we had hoped. Actually, that already became evident shortly before the end of the war. For example, in 1961 or 1962 I took part in a summer academy of the National Liberation Front (FLN) to train teachers for the future Algeria. Most people taught physics or mathematics, but I was to deal with cultural topics. I arrived there with a few books by Algerian writers, I forget which ones, and people from the FLN said to me, 'No, we don't want those authors!' So, the FLN wasn't that open after all! Along with these experiences, another important event – at least, for those who already saw themselves as philosophers – was the publication of the first books by Althusser. For me, somewhat earlier, another aspect was also a factor: *Clarté*, a communist magazine for students, once featured a section on the concept of alienation. That's a very important memory for me, because that was the first time I realized that the notion of alienation presupposes the prior existence of a non-alienated state.

Peter Engelmann: A state of unity, of not being alien.

Jean-Luc Nancy: Yes. This memory is only a very small piece of the puzzle within a whole process, a gradual questioning of Marxism, revolution and also the notion of progress in history. We weren't aware that Foucault, around the same time, was giving lectures in which he stated that the epoch of history had given way to the age of space. So, one could say that we were part of that movement without viewing it as a movement. But we certainly understood that the communist party, and anything that called itself communist, was a dead end. Anything that declared itself as being on the extreme left or Maoist was dubious for us. Philippe had been involved in the group *Socialisme ou barbarie* for a while, he was still living in Bordeaux then. There he met

Jean-François Lyotard, but didn't see him after that until we were in Strasbourg together.

Peter Engelmann: It was a group of undogmatic Marxists.

Jean-Luc Nancy: Yes, but we too went through many internal crises. For my part, I remember that I subscribed to *Le Quotidien du Peuple* in 1966 and 1967, a Maoist journal, directly from Peking. But I didn't find those Maoist things so interesting. For a while I was a member of the PSU, the *Parti socialiste unifié*. The old *Parti socialiste* had fallen apart; it had split up into the UGS (*Union de la gauche socialiste*) and the PSA, the *Parti socialiste autonome*. Then the PSU in turn emerged from these two parties. The PSU struck me as a new way to be neither a communist nor a Maoist nor a Trotskyist. But a year in the party was enough for me. I didn't like it.

Peter Engelmann: So, the essence of your criticism of the communist or leftist parties was that they were dogmatic, that they were cadre parties which installed themselves as new powers but didn't bring any freedom?

Jean-Luc Nancy: I think that was just one side, and not the most significant one. The other side was the intellectual or spiritual one. The feeling that there wasn't really anything new to find here, no new worldview, if you like. In 1962 *Esprit* had organized a conference dealing with the question: why is the young generation silent? I gave a lecture there and said something like this: 'We are silent because we have nothing to do with the grand notions of the history of progress. We don't believe in them any more. We need something different, even if we don't know what that is yet. And we don't have any use for religion in its institutionalized form any more either, whether it's the Protestant or the Catholic Church.' For a while, we saw the Israeli kibbutz as a model for something new, a new form of coexistence, neither capitalist nor communist, a socialist project, but not tied to the notion of a great historical process. I hardly knew any Jews, but somehow I'd heard about the idea. It was only much later that I saw Chris Marker's film *Description of a Struggle*, which shows how Israel resisted the tendency to become a capitalist country, and ultimately failed. So we ended up without any model, any example.

II

History: Between Process and Event

Peter Engelmann: Let me try to summarize. This whole setting of practical experiences and theoretical reflections that you've described led to an increasing distance between you and communism. And you were looking for different forms of community, of coexistence, for social alternatives.

Jean-Luc Nancy: We felt a lack of community, even though we lived in a society that seemed quite healthy at the time. There were no economic problems – on the contrary, it was the period of *Les Trente Glorieuses*,² the years of the French economic miracle. But we lacked perspective. And at the same time we were reading books by Althusser, Deleuze ...

Peter Engelmann: And you agreed with their critique?

Jean-Luc Nancy: Yes, but above all, there was something new in these books. They opened up a different way of thinking. It's difficult to reconstruct the exact chronology .... At any rate, I felt most clearly – though not for the first time – that something new was beginning when I read *Voice and Phenomenon* by Derrida.[3]

Peter Engelmann: So, it was neither structural Marxism nor Deleuze, but rather Derrida. That was the point.

Jean-Luc Nancy: I remember that Philippe and I started talking about Derrida very soon at our meetings. Heidegger and Derrida, those were the two reference points. Naturally we also read *Of Grammatology*,[4] but for me it was above all *Voice and Phenomenon* that was a decisive event, specifically the passage where he writes that the inner voice of the consciousness speaks or speaks silently, that this moment takes a certain time, perhaps only a very short time, but a time nonetheless. In French he writes *une durée* – a duration. And this *durée* is the content of *diffé-rance*. I remember this passage very precisely, because this idea was like the rebirth of Hegel for me. Certainly, I was very strongly influenced by Hegel, absolutely not the systematic Hegel of the *Science of Logic*, but quite the opposite: a Hegel of openness, of consciousness's coming-outside-oneself, its stepping-outside-itself, and so forth. Strangely enough, I came into contact with Hegel's philosophy through a Jesuit, around 1960, 1961, after a friend had drawn my attention to his Hegel seminar. That was wonderful, my first philosophical infatuation. Since then I've always felt connected to Hegel, in different ways.

Peter Engelmann: Did you deal with the *Phenomenology of Spirit*[5] there?

Jean-Luc Nancy: Yes, especially the *Phenomenology*. At the end of the *Phenomenology* there's a slightly altered Schiller quotation: 'from the chalice of this realm of spirits foams forth for Him his own infinitude'.[6] That became a kind of motto for me. I suppose that in this foam, I had found what I needed for the first time. And this foaming, this excess, was what I found again in the *durée* of the moment in Derrida.

Peter Engelmann: So, one could say that this experience marked your philosophical awakening, and has informed your philosophical work since then?

Jean-Luc Nancy: Yes. Then I came across Heidegger, probably in 1961 or 1962, again through a friend, a student of Beaufret. At first I didn't understand Heidegger at all. He gave me the *Letter on Humanism*,[7] and I laughed, and said, 'What's all this about the shepherd of Being?' At the same time, there was a statement that had a strong effect on me, namely that humanism doesn't value the *humanitas* of humans highly enough. That was very important for me. When I read that I thought, 'Yes, the man is right!' I think to me it was a repetition of Pascal's dictum: man finally surpasses man. Perhaps it was because of my religious background that the idea that *humanitas* goes infinitely beyond humans felt intuitively right. But Heidegger was concerned with more than that. When I read those words by Heidegger, I had no idea of his involvement in National Socialism, really none at all! Until then I had never heard of Heidegger, I didn't even know his name. I probably had the impression of recognizing something familiar in that statement. At first I sensed a sort of kinship with what I'd encountered in Derrida as the moment and in Hegel as foam. In addition, it showed a sensitivity to a certain emptiness in humanism. There had been so much talk of humanism, and I had started to feel that this word was moving completely in isolation, it had no content. Obviously one's a humanist, how can one not be a humanist! Whether one's a Christian, Marxist, phenomenologist … one's always a humanist. I remember that in my final year at the university I had to write a text on Sartre's essay *Is Existentialism a Humanism?*[8] And Roger Garaudy, who later converted to Islam, wrote a book about Marxism as humanism. The communists also claimed humanism for themselves.

Peter Engelmann: Yes! Amazingly, that was a very important book for the opposition in the GDR, precisely because it introduced humanism into the discussion on communism.

In the GDR it was the critique of actually existing socialism that took place in the name of humanism.

Jean-Luc Nancy: At any rate, everyone considers themselves a humanist. And suddenly Heidegger says that previous humanist interpretations of humans did not value the essence of humans – and he uses the Latin word *humanitas* – highly enough. In my memory, it's about this height. I had a feeling of sublimity that's absent from the usual situation of contemporary thought. So, my first encounter with Heidegger was very ambiguous; on the one hand, I found this sublimity or tone of being sublime funny, for example, when he speaks of the shepherd of Being, but on the other hand, I took him completely seriously where he deals with the *humanitas* of humans. Then I read more Heidegger, I only read *Being and Time*[9] much later. Today I would say that this mystical understanding of history unfolding as destiny [*Geschick*] in *Being and Time* marks the politically neuralgic point in his philosophy. Without the assumption of destiny, without a conception of history as destiny, Heidegger would never have become a Nazi.

Peter Engelmann: So, Heidegger's Nazi involvement is already implicit in the logic of his understanding of history as destiny?

Jean-Luc Nancy: In my opinion, one can see that very clearly in *Being and Time*. Specifically, where Heidegger writes about history, historicity and destiny, starting around §72. That's the decisive point, it's where everything changes. Because now one learns that the finite Dasein of the individual is only fateful, and can only become destined if it goes into battle for the people [*Volk*].

Peter Engelmann: That's already the model for his political involvement.

Jean-Luc Nancy: That's the model, of course. I think the point is that destiny needs the common, the With. The With is the decisive aspect. Heidegger already introduces it very early, around §26, where he explains that the Being-with [*Mitsein*] of Dasein is an existential, not only categorical. But after that, Heidegger only occasionally speaks of this With, there's no comprehensive analysis of Being-with in Heidegger. Only in his reflections on history, on historicity, does one learn that one finds one's own 'with' [*Mit*] in the community. And the community is what it is, in the battle for the people, because the people are or present a historical and destined entity. And that changes almost everything.

Peter Engelmann: Is that an example of an ideological anticipation of a totalitarian, political structure?

Jean-Luc Nancy: Yes, of course!

Peter Engelmann: So, you would say that there are thought figures which at least anticipate and legitimate a totalitarian political system ...

Jean-Luc Nancy: Yes, and I would even say that I've occupied myself more and more intensively with it. It's the question of history, one can expound it quite well using *Being and Time*. As long as there is no reference to history in *Being and Time*, one could think that there is no reason to address the problem of history again, and if there is, then one has to pose the question in terms of history as a process or history as an event. It's actually hard to understand why Heidegger is thinking in the direction of a process. Well, naturally this view of history has prominent exponents in the history of philosophy, think of Kant, Herder, Hegel … Especially in the German tradition, one finds the notion of history as progress, that is, as a teleological process, and thus as something that functions precisely *without* Hegel's foam.

Peter Engelmann: Essentially a deterministic process.

Jean-Luc Nancy: Yes, and foam rather aims at an excess: there is no end.

Peter Engelmann: Excess as the unforeseeable, the uncontrollable, the unexpected, the event.

Jean-Luc Nancy: Yes, event, of course. I take up the word 'event' because it plays such an important part in Heidegger slightly later on. Nowadays we can no longer understand how the schema of a process and a teleology can have such a strong effect. Naturally it's far more complicated in Heidegger, and later he moved very far away from it. He spoke of the destiny of the occident, but naturally he didn't say that he could imagine the end of that process. Nonetheless, there is a notion of telos in Heidegger, namely in the form of the idea and the prospect that a true relationship with Being can be attained. At the end of 'Anaximander's Saying',[10] he writes that perhaps the occidental catastrophe will be reversed, and the oblivion of Being will be or enable a recovery of Being. In my view that's irreconcilable with his warning not to forget that there is no *one* Being, that the *one* Being does not exist, that we can never speak of the *one* Being. That's the argumentation he develops with reference to the event or en-owning [*Ereignis*] when he speaks of appropriating [*Ereignen*], dis-owning [*Ent-eignung*], dedication [*Zueignung*] and so on. For me, this is where Heidegger's real point lies. But, on the opposite side, the side of history as destiny, oblivion of Being and so on, one returns to the process and the telos, even if Heidegger rejected the notion of a final purpose. For me this is not only a problematic area in Heidegger, but actually a pressing question for all of us today: how can we conceive of history as non-processual and non-teleological? I think Foucault was one of the first to take steps in this direction. And I think that with the word *destinerrance*,[11] Derrida found something that operates precisely on the reverse of Heidegger. It means destiny, *destin*, but destiny as *errance*, as aimless wandering. Incidentally, there's a Heidegger feature in the next issue of *Le Monde*, and I contributed an article to that in which I develop precisely this argument, namely that Derrida's word *destinerrance* is a way to depart from Heidegger's thought where it remains tied to teleology. But one also has to take into account that Heidegger only conceived of history as destiny, and not also *errance*, during a certain time – roughly from 1939 to 1942. In other words, Heidegger could only have understood the errancy of *errance* as error at that time. To the extent that Heidegger poses the question of Being in a radical fashion, however, his thought remains *the* philosophical event of the twentieth century for me. I don't see how one could think any differently. The question of the happening, the occurrence of history is our question too. I've already mentioned Foucault – why did he develop his whole reflection on history if not because he picked up something from Heidegger that's precisely *not* connected to destiny, but in a certain sense far more to what Derrida called *destinerrance*? But the figure of *destinerrance* preserves something of destiny [*Geschick*], and perhaps it's not possible here to dismiss this conception of a sending [*Schicken*], but certainly the notion of a telos. This throws up an incredibly serious metaphysical and even anthropological question, because it seems impossible, from today's perspective, *not* to view history as a process, as we see that a history which began with the Greeks truly became the history of the world.

Peter Engelmann: You mean, from today's perspective, history actually presents itself as a process?

Jean-Luc Nancy: Yes. What are the Chinese doing today? They're doing everything we are: capitalism, computer science. Africa is perhaps the only continent that hasn't really joined in yet, or only to a minor extent. Nonetheless, it seems there is only one rationality ...

Peter Engelmann: ... and it's getting globalized. In that sense it's a process.

Jean-Luc Nancy: Yes, because globalization didn't just follow by chance from a beginning, it's already inherent in the essence of the beginning. In the form of Christianity, for example, of universal religion, universal equality. In Marx, this equality takes the form of general equivalence. The capitalist system was invented as a way of forming a universe.

Peter Engelmann: That's the logic of capital.

Jean-Luc Nancy: In my view, it's connected to something one could call the regime of production. In the fourteenth century there was a major shift in Europe. For example, the coin production trade changed fundamentally: it was no longer just a matter of producing money for a prince's household, but also for trading, and about trading in such a way that one could always turn money into more money, which resulted in the monetary economy, money-lending with interest, and so on. The history of anti-Semitism is intimately connected to this. In Marxian thought, this production is expanded to include human life: human life is its own production as social production. On the one hand, that means the complete liberation or autonomization of humans from the context of nature – man as a creator.

Peter Engelmann: An anti-religious, anti-theological stance.

Jean-Luc Nancy: On the other hand, this subsumes everything under the order of production. And this means that something is endangered, forgotten or lost, namely *reproduction*. Before this regime of production, humanity lived in highly varied forms of a reproduction of life. People cultivated this and that to continue living, but they didn't try to produce a different life. Even in as great a civilization as China, the order of reproduction was maintained, even if the forms of culture, art and thought very gradually changed. Nonetheless, China seems like a model case of reproduction, because it was there that this form of life took on the largest proportions and persisted the longest. That's why some people consider China's current situation a disaster: the old China has disappeared, but nothing new has replaced it.

Peter Engelmann: That means there's a form of society that reproduces itself, economically too, but doesn't pursue any further goals. And then comes capitalist production, which is not only a production of surplus value, but also a self-design in regard to a different form, a different form of community, a different society. And the idea of communism is also one of these models that belongs to productive, not reproductive forms of economy and coexistence. Is that what you mean?

Jean-Luc Nancy: Yes. Regarding communism, perhaps one should point out first of all that the word 'communism', historically speaking, comes from Christianity. In Catholic Church law, a communist good was one that belonged to the community, not to one person. The word 'communism' then appears for the first time in the writings of Restif de la Bretonne – a contemporary of Rousseau, tellingly enough, who aims to provide a comprehensive overview of political governmental forms, and refers to the first form of society as communism, only practised by two tribes on the Pacific coast of South America, where people do everything together; they work together in the morning and have fun together in the afternoon. That's his entire description of communism!

Peter Engelmann: But that's exactly what Marx writes in *The Communist Manifesto*!

Jean-Luc Nancy: Yes, of course. It's really wonderful! I don't know if Marx knew that text by Restif. But I don't think it's a coincidence that Restif uses the word 'communism'; I'd say it expresses a longing. It articulates the awareness that society – society at the end of the eighteenth century – is lacking something, namely a communal spirit. That's nothing amazing, since the whole of political theory, political and social thought, already took the individual as its point of departure two or three centuries earlier. Hobbes, Locke, von Pufendorf, whoever. They always begin with the one, followed by the question of how to bring together the different individuals. And how one can make it possible for them to live together. This is precisely the question that no one asked in the Middle Ages, because – to put it very simply – the way people lived together was predetermined: they lived together first of all because they were all God's children, and secondly, because everyone had a social rank assigned to them in the feudal system. In a sense, feudalism is a cosmos of its own. The peasants farmed the land and bred livestock so that their ruler would have something to eat, and in return the ruler gave the peasants protection. The strict notions of honour – think of the oath of fealty, for example – can be interpreted as a way of developing a sacrality of society as such. This secular system wasn't Christian at first, it was only interpreted in Christian terms later: we are all God's subjects. This results in an addition: Christianity, which initially lacked a model for life in this world, was given a model for earthly life in the shape of feudalism. Conversely, feudalism found its religious legitimation in Christianity. Perhaps this is why Carl Schmitt argues that all our political concepts are secularized concepts.

Peter Engelmann: Feudalism as Christianity for the mortal world, as it were? (*Laughs*)

Jean-Luc Nancy: But the pre-modern world already took a direction that destroyed precisely *that*, because history became the history of those who *didn't* want to stay in that sacred system, but demanded a complete autonomy of the state. This characterizes the whole of modern state theory, the theory of sovereignty of Jean Bodin and others, perhaps one even has to include Machiavelli too. And it's connected to the memory of the Roman Empire, which was always present. In a sense, Europe always wanted to found a new Rome. Rome is the only case in history in which a civil religion truly existed. Rome was neither the city nor the state, Rome was Rome. One could say that Rome was its own goddess. Perhaps that's why Rome was a society where gods were everywhere, where every action requires a religious action first. Christianity established itself because the substance of this civil religion ultimately disappeared. Why it did so is another matter.

Peter Engelmann: What are you referring to as the substance of this civil religion?

Jean-Luc Nancy: By substance I mean that Rome could always imagine itself as something that hadn't existed before then, namely *as* the world. Unlike Athens, Sparta or Carthage, for example,

Rome wasn't tied to a particular ethnicity or locality. Rome founded and justified itself. Hence the legend that Rome had kings, but could dethrone them. Rome was the invention of law. Here law is both a means and an end: if one was subject to Roman law, one was a Roman. Saint Paul is the perfect example. When he was taken captive by the Romans, he invoked his Roman civil rights, that is, he asserted his legal right to be tried by a Roman court as a Roman citizen.

Peter Engelmann: So, Rome means the invention of the world as a state under the rule of law?

Jean-Luc Nancy: Yes, exactly.

Peter Engelmann: Human coexistence is based on a system of law that no longer requires any justification and has no preconditions. And this law is the law of the world. But now, one or two centuries BCE, a certain sadness spreads among all these Mediterranean peoples; Freud refers to this at the end of *Moses and Monotheism*[12] when he speaks of a general unease and premonition of disaster, invoking the historiography of his time. This would mean that something became unbearable for all the peoples of the Roman Empire. But what, and why? I don't have an explanation, but we do know that there must have been an immense religious need, because there were more religions in the Roman Empire during the first two centuries BCE than at any previous time anywhere ...

Peter Engelmann: You mean that this sadness came from a lack, that this world as a state of law was missing something?

Jean-Luc Nancy: Yes, exactly. And it seems to me that one can also tie this lack to the Stoics and the Epicureans. It relates to what Foucault called care of the self. It's already a symptom, because what does care of the self mean? It comes from the feeling that one's lost in the world. One doesn't know where this world is going. The question of fate became a central question for Stoics at that time: how can I gain knowledge of my fate? And what can I do if I am denied it? The Epicurean doctrine, on the other hand, states that you shouldn't worry about that, you should simply live in the way that causes you least discomfort or pain. So, the two centuries before Christ were genuinely dominated by something disturbing, something unpleasant. People no longer knew how to act in life as human beings.

Peter Engelmann: And Christianity entered this situation as an offer of meaning?

Jean-Luc Nancy: No, I'd actually say that Christianity is a product of that situation! First of all, Christianity was an inner transformation or reformation of Judaism. I find Jan Assmann very convincing when he argues that the history of the Jews is the history of the attempt to separate human salvation from worldly rule: the Jews were slaves of Pharaoh, they left Egypt, founded a Jewish kingdom, but soon there were internal divisions and also the separation of king and prophet. The prophet became a critic of the king. This led to the doctrine of the messiah, which means 'anointed one' and initially referred exclusively to the king, and was only used to refer to the prophet later on. The entire history of messianism is at once the history of the messiah who will perhaps never come and the history of the increasing separation or distinction between the religious and the political order.

So Judaism split into two: rabbinical Judaism and Christianity. Incipient Christianity was then a movement of an inner transformation of Judaism as a renewed liberation from oneself, from political order. Recall the words Christ speaks to Pilate: 'My kingdom is not of this world.' So, at the time when Rome seemed too much like a world, a second world burst in. From that point one could say, 'I'm *in* this world, but I'm not *of* this world.' With Saint Augustine there are two kingdoms, two *civitates*. And from this perspective, the history of communism can be read as the history of the reunification of these two worlds, the overcoming of this schism.

Peter Engelmann: You say that Christianity created a second world.

Jean-Luc Nancy: Until roughly the time of Charlemagne, Christians had the expectation that the second world would come, and with it the end of this world. Gradually Christians realized that the end wouldn't come, and subsequently started thinking about how they might be able and allowed to live in *this* world in order to preserve the possibility of the second world.

But there was always an ambivalence: will this world come later, or does it already exist now? Throughout the entire history of Christianity, both ideas are always there. The mystics lived in the awareness that the second world was already here. Other thinkers remained faithful to the traditional religious view that a second, eternal life begins in heaven after death. This question is complicated by the Last Judgement, because one can't easily see from a worldly perspective how the end of history can come. And this is what the Reformation, what Protestantism addresses, think of Weber's thesis about the connection between Protestant ethics and the emergence of capitalism. But here one can also refer to the Franciscans. Giacomo Todeschini shows in his book *Franciscan Wealth*[13] how the Franciscans contributed to the genesis of capitalism – which doesn't imply that they wanted a capitalist form of life. For the Franciscans, the whole issue of poverty really meant just that one shouldn't use wealth for oneself, one has to use it for the good of all. It was a doctrine of use: wealth must be used for the common good, one has to take away the wealth of the rich and give it to the people. And 'people' essentially meant citizens at that time. I think this can help us to see more clearly how capitalism comes partly from this Christian idea of a good use of this world in order to reconcile it with the second world.

III

The Ontology of Communality

Peter Engelmann: Let's return specifically to Strasbourg. Can you say a little more about your collaboration with Philippe, which was a very special kind of collaboration?

Jean-Luc Nancy: I met Philippe in 1967. And it was during the events of 1968 that everything happened between us too: we decided to stay in Strasbourg, and at the same time we began a chiastic personal history. Ultimately, Philippe got together with my first wife and I had children with Philippe's wife. At first I was still living in Colmar, but after a very serious car accident in late 1969 – I crashed between Strasbourg and Colmar, breaking my hip – I decided to move to Strasbourg. And with that, an important aspect of the whole thing began: living together.

Peter Engelmann: The four of you all lived together?

Jean-Luc Nancy: Yes, the four of us as well as our four children. That was connected to the sexual freedom of the 1968 generation, which my first wife and I had already lived before. And also, of course, to the subject of community: living together. And this communal life was connected to our living and thinking together at the university. By October 1968 everything was more or less over, everything returned to normal, one could say. But in Strasbourg, at least, every-thing was still in upheaval. So, Philippe and I had started the year very much as usual, but we and the students wanted to deal with completely new content. So, we simultaneously continued with classical topics and also discussed entirely new things – structuralism, Lacan, Foucault, Derrida and so forth. And students came who wanted to work on that. So very soon we started organizing something outside the normal courses, together with colleagues from other subjects like literature, history, at times there were a few psychoanalysts too. We called them 'seminars', which wasn't the norm in French universities back then. And we started studying Bataille. I don't remember exactly why, but Philippe and I could agree on that, we wanted to start with him. Naturally, Bataille's thought was absent from the university. In the following years we held the seminar more or less every Saturday, each year with a different topic and with several people we had invited. The seminars were always very well attended. We had almost no money, but ultimately we could always scrape together enough to pay for a few trips and the like. Strangely enough, hardly anything from those seminars has been published; although we wrote a lot of texts, they were never made into books. At the same time as holding the seminars on Bataille, we also organized a conference on rhetoric to which we invited Derrida, Lyotard and Genette.

Peter Engelmann: That was in 1969, wasn't it?

Jean-Luc Nancy: Yes, in the autumn. A year earlier we had started doing Bataille and I had written

42

a short, very naive text, a kind of panorama of current philosophy, heavily influenced by epistemology, specifically by Canguilhem, who was an important figure for myself and my generation. In any case, I tried in that text to contrast this interest in science, which was very much in fashion at the time, with a philosophical interest of the kind I had found in Derrida especially. It was also about the question of whether a new form of science was possible. That's also what Derrida asks in *Of Grammatology*: is this a new science, is it an *-ology*, a parody or a metaphor? This text of mine was published in the university newspaper along with various other articles. And I sent it to Derrida, at the École Normale, because I didn't have his private address. During the course of the year he replied, and I was very moved, because he wrote that he had already read some of my articles that were published in *Esprit* and thought that we would meet at some point. That's how it all started. So, then we organized this conference on rhetoric and Derrida came; he gave a lecture that was later published as 'White Mythology'.[14] Genette also came, as he'd been one of Philippe's teachers in Le Mans. We had also invited Lyotard, whom

Philippe still knew from *Socialisme ou barbarie*, though we weren't in contact with him and didn't know anything about his activities at that time. But his wife, like Philippe's, was an English teacher at the University of Strasbourg, and that was how we found out that he was also interested in rhetoric. So we invited him too, and he came.

Peter Engelmann: So everyone came together at this conference?

Jean-Luc Nancy: Yes, though it was just for two days. The theme of the conference, rhetoric, came from Philippe. It wasn't really my topic at all, but through Philippe I'd developed an interest in literature in the broadest sense, and also in rhetoric. So we already had an idea of what would later be termed the 'linguistic turn'. We wanted to occupy ourselves with language, with the sign, and so we founded the *Groupe de recherche sur le théorie du signe et du texte*.

Peter Engelmann: You hit the bullseye there: that's been the central subject ever since. Was Derrida also part of it?

Jean-Luc Nancy: No, Philippe and I were in close contact with him, but the *Groupe* consisted only of colleagues from Strasbourg who wanted to join in. Then we invited speakers, naturally Derrida and Lyotard, but also Roland Barthes, Tzvetan Todorov, Jean-Joseph Goux and others.

Peter Engelmann: Did you also invite Sarah Kofman?

Jean-Luc Nancy: Yes, of course. We had met her through Jacques.

Peter Engelmann: Let's go back to the events of 1968 and talk about what set off those events.

Jean-Luc Nancy: Yes, you're right, we should look a little more closely at 1968. Because, unlike in Paris, the situation in Strasbourg wasn't so much a confrontation in the street as a way of gathering at the university. Hundreds of us sat in this beautiful old German imperial university, debating hour after hour. For us it was less about a particular political action than about a way of keeping the entire realm of politics in limbo: a suspension of politics. Naturally political involvement played a part for us too, and we had connections to political movements in other countries. But the main thing was to be together, to have discussions. Obviously, there were people in Strasbourg too who wanted to change something, and for most of them that meant founding a critical university, but that was exactly what we didn't want. I remember very well the day we went to see a committee for a critical university. After half an hour we decided: we're not joining in. For us it wasn't about a new politics, it was about withdrawing and seeing what's at stake in the current situation. We didn't see any potential for something new in the political directions of the time, whether communist, far left or Trotskyist. And we felt very soon that the reshaping of the university, which was seemingly the main motive and purpose of the entire movement, was simply an adaptation of the university to something we didn't have a name for back then, but which was something resembling consumer society. We knew all too well that the reforms enacted by the government would only lead to a co-optation of the movement.

Peter Engelmann: If I understand you correctly, you and the others sensed that both the political demands of the students and the measures subsequently implemented by the government wouldn't lead to any substantial change, that it was simply a matter of system-immanent adjustments, and that this approach didn't hold the potential for a real change. And that was why you wanted to question and reflect fundamentally on this system, and based on that you would look for alternatives?

Jean-Luc Nancy: Yes. Philippe and I wanted to do work on politics, we held the view that we needed to rethink the political. For myself especially, that increasingly came down to the question of society or community.

Peter Engelmann: So, the question of community or society came about through a reformulation of the concept of politics? Or was it more of a rupture, an abandonment of the concept of politics, a change of terminology?

Jean-Luc Nancy: No, more of a reformulation. This was accompanied firstly by an interest in literature. Not as an interest in fictions; our point of departure was rather the question of how far literature calls philosophy into question as a system, as a conceptual system. What is the relationship between literature and philosophy, how does literature find its way into philosophy? Literature is something that's given to others to read, and which stands within a horizon of communication from the start. In philosophy, things are seemingly different. Philosophy presents itself as the intimacy of thought; hence the question of how to practise philosophy. What is the question of theatre? What does the question of theatre, especially Greek tragedy, have to do with philosophy? Plato composed tragedies in his youth, and supposedly burned them later in order to write dialogues instead. These things were very much on our minds in those years. As was, naturally, the literature of Romanticism. Philippe and I published *The Literary Absolute*[15] on that in 1978. The idea was of an infinite literature as the epitome of a new society, a new form of coexistence. Naturally, the way of life of the Jena Circle, the early Romantics around the Schlegel brothers, was significant for this idea of society. Somebody once said mockingly, 'those people in Strasbourg are like the ones in Jena, the women knit socks while the men chat'. (*Laughs*)

But, naturally, it was also about reshaping sexual relationships. For a while, some people thought Philippe and I were homosexual. Later we heard that someone had said about us, 'Oh, the poor women, having to live like that with the men!' That's not just an anecdote, it relates to the question of what coexistence means. It's about the ontology of coexistence, of being together. Secondly, it was important for us to ask where one could find a way of thinking coexistence outside of philosophy. Because philosophy always started from the individual and conceived of coexistence from there. What was missing was the opposite approach, an attempt to begin with coexistence. And this realization led us to Freud.

Peter Engelmann: So you both wanted a change of perspective: to begin with the community, rather than start with the individual and move on to the community from there?

Jean-Luc Nancy: Yes. And who begins before the individual if not Freud! That was how we saw it, at least. But, ultimately, we were disappointed, in part at least, because our experience was that it's very difficult to find anything in Freud that starts substantially before the individual. Philippe and I wrote two texts together about that: 'La panique politique'[16] and 'The Jewish People Do Not Dream'.[17] We wrote the latter for a conference on psychoanalysis. It deals with the fact that the Jewish people may be a people without a myth, in the sense of the Greek myth. And that maybe one could find some way here to envisage a community without any myth. Naturally that was connected to the question of the Nazi myth, on which we wrote a little book around the same time.[18] Those were different attempts to find a beginning located *before* or *outside* the individual. It was no coincidence that we read Bataille with the students for a whole year at the time. We'd already dealt with Bataille before that, but more in the context of our studies in literature. At any rate, I had noticed during my reading that there were various reflections on community in Bataille which I wanted to take up.

Peter Engelmann: What year was that?

Jean-Luc Nancy: That was 1981, 1982. And in the spring of 1982, Jean Christophe Bailly suggested devoting an issue of his journal *Aléa* to this subject, and chose the title *La communauté, le nombre*. Jean Christophe always finds the right words, and that formulation was absolutely on the mark and greatly inspired me: *le nombre* refers to pure quantity, the number of individuals. *La communauté* was a term that I'd previously only found in Bataille, nowhere else. It comes from the same root as *communisme*, but without the suffix. What does that mean? I immediately wanted to write something about it, and in the spring of 1983 my text appeared in *Aléa* together with other articles on this subject, then later again as the first chapter of my book *The Inoperative Community*,[19] published the same year. One sign that this subject genuinely had something to do with that time was that, in November of the same year, Blanchot published *The Unavowable Community*.[20] Recently, I reconstructed the whole chronology. In the spring of 1983, Blanchot wrote an article for *Le nouveau commerce* devoted to Levinas. In it, Blanchot conveyed to Levinas that he offered a different form of relationship with the other to that of Levinas, not a relationship of responsibility but one of passion. And Blanchot explains that with reference to the novella *The Malady of*

Death[21] by Marguerite Duras. Blanchot also refers to Bataille here, and speaks of *la communauté des amants* – the community of lovers. And, evidently, Blanchot was already correcting the proofs of his article when he received my one from *Aléa*. And so there's a footnote at the very end of his text in which he refers to my article as important work on Bataille. There wasn't time for more. Then, in the summer, he wrote *The Unavowable Community*. He rewrote the first half of the book, with references to Bataille and a critique of my reading of Bataille, which culminated more or less in the claim that I hadn't read Bataille properly. But the second part is his article on Levinas from *Le nouveau commerce*, the same text, but with around ten pages added at the beginning and the end dealing with the subject of community. So, what had only been described as the relationship with the other as passion in the first version becomes, in this book, the question of how to think community. And Blanchot concludes that one must not define community as such. I tried to explain that in my last book *The Inoperative Community*. It's very complicated. Because what's behind it is something that's also part of this whole story: in his book *The Unavowable Community*, Blanchot reveals himself as a non-democrat, albeit in a concealed way. He also did that a year later in *Les intellectuels en question*.[22] What he means is that democracy as a pure gathering of individuals does not create a community. Community is something that must never be founded, organized or instituted. Community is something that occurs against the background of a non-occurrence, as in the story by Duras: the man and the woman in Duras's story don't love each other, they reach an agreement; only the woman knows pleasure in the sense of going-into-the-infinite. But it's too complicated. Unfortunately I can't go into that properly now … (*Laughs*) Anyway, I didn't understand that book by Blanchot at the time. But what increasingly amazed me was that no one really wanted to understand the book! Not even Jacques. Or Philippe. Nonetheless: in Blanchot's reading, the woman in the story becomes Duras's Christ. She gives her body to the man as Christ gave us his body, in an immemorial way. So here Blanchot characterizes Christ's gift as immemorial, and this is connected to earlier texts, in which he states that mystical experience constitutes an experience in which the subject is not aware of this experience (which is not the same as an experience without a subject). I think that's the essence of Blanchot's thesis. This means that one needs something like a myth in order to represent it. And he speaks decidedly of myth in his text; he writes that the body of the woman is mythical. And the woman seems to become a myth through her transformation into Christ. And Blanchot really takes responsibility for this interpretation: the gift of the body and the disappearance of the woman are compared quite explicitly to the death of Christ. Furthermore, Blanchot cites the story of Jesus on the road to Emmaus and compares the man in the story to Christ's disciples: in the same way that they are only able to recognize Christ as their saviour once he has died as a man, the man can only recognize the woman once she is gone. What is Blanchot telling us here about community? That community only reveals itself once it is no longer present. Though it was never actually present in the true sense, only as the enjoyment of the woman, who ultimately disappears. So, not only is the subject of the experience of togetherness not present; in mythical fashion, it is located in a form of sublime *absentia* which Blanchot subsequently tells us is actually literature itself. One can see from this that something has remained of the Blanchot of the 1930s. I mean his view of myth, which naturally also has a political thrust – though not in the sense of the Nazi myth, of course. I don't think that Blanchot was ever a Nazi, nor was he a fascist, but he was certainly very far to the Right. And there was a part of that which he never abandoned, as he always insisted that something like a transcendent could be … Perhaps for him it's literature itself that plays this part. In my book I try to show this – so: he takes a writer's story as his topic. But he speaks about it in a way which conveys that although he is not the author of the story, he gradually becomes the author of the truth of this story. Thus, Blanchot takes the place of Duras, in a sense. He also writes that the author Duras must somehow be personally involved in such a story. For Blanchot it's probably also a reminder of 1968. He speaks of 1968 as the time in which perhaps, just once, an extremely ephemeral community formed – or rather non-formed – in the streets. We know that he took part in a few political activities at the time. Perhaps he also had a brief relationship with Duras. In any case, his book includes a kind of identification between the self, i.e. Blanchot, and Duras, the writer. And as for the title of his text, *The Unavowable Community*, I think this 'unavowable' suggests, 'Yes, there is something to avow. But I avow nothing. It's up to you to understand this, be clever!' I'm tempted to say that this 'avowing/not avowing' is perhaps, in an uncanny way, at the basis of every sincere allegiance *to* democracy. Because this allegiance can't be a recognition of a pre-existing sense, nor can one simply give democracy a sense – that of a 'real' togetherness or a 'real' equality, for example. So I tried to read the book very closely. After its publication in 1983, no one spoke about the book in detail any more, even though it was often quoted. The question is, why? For our part, it may be because we were occupied with setting up the *Centre de recherches philosophiques sur le politique* at the time.

Peter Engelmann: You founded that in Paris in 1981.

Jean-Luc Nancy: Exactly, on Jacques's recommendation. He had told us, 'If you want, I could get funds from the École Normale to found a research centre. You could do whatever you want.' And we said, 'Then we'll do something on the question of the political.' That was the logical consequence of everything we had done before then. We located this centre in the horizon of a particular motif that we called the *retrait du politique*. To this day, I find it very difficult to make the double meaning of *retrait* clear. It refers both to the question of retreating the political and to the demand to retrace, to re-enact the political. There was a lot of movement during the existence of the centre, both politically and theoretically. Theoretically speaking, we all agreed at the start that we were dealing with a retreat of the political. But a number of very different approaches developed from that. Luc Ferry, for example, argued that today, politics is concentrated in the question of human rights. There was disagreement, we held the opinion that something else was needed. And then Solidarność was founded, the protest movement against the political rulers and the communist system in Poland. This led to the question of civil society. Solidarność is perhaps the birthplace of the phrase 'civil society' that is so common today. Civil society ias something that has nothing to do with the state, which exists perhaps not *against*, but certainly outside the state and the political institutions. That's actually rather strange, because, historically speaking, civil society always meant political society. But, in Poland, for a certain time, there was indeed this opposition: Solidarność on the one side, the state on the other. People held the view that foreign policy, the army, was part of the state, but social institutions belonged to civil society. This opened up a rupture within the centre, because some found this concept of civil society very interesting – especially Lyotard – while others rejected the approach because they felt it risked a loss of politics.

Peter Engelmann: What kind of activities were there at the centre? Were there conferences or regular meetings?

Jean-Luc Nancy: We met regularly, roughly once a month, there was a lecture with a subsequent discussion, or sometimes just a discussion on a particular topic.

Peter Engelmann: And the people at the centre were Philippe, you, Jacques, Jean-François ...

Jean-Luc Nancy: Yes, and also Rancière, Badiou, Balibar, Ferry, Lefort … There were around thirty or forty people who participated regularly. Sarah Kofman too, for example, but she never gave a lecture as far as I can recall. Neither did Jacques, in fact! The only time Jacques spoke at the centre was when he told us about his meeting with the dissidents of Charta 77 after the suppression of the Prague Spring and his time in prison over there. But the centre's work wasn't in line with Derrida's politics. That's a very interesting question, because naturally Philippe and I asked him repeatedly if he could finally give a lecture. But his response to these invitations was always vague, and he would put us off until another time. I think he didn't want to at that time, also in the political context of the centre. He didn't want to take a political stance, especially not on the matter of civil society. So he waited until a few years later, when he finally published *Politics of Friendship*,[23] where this politics – politics in the plural – of friendship also goes beyond politics, one could say, and aims for a new concept of the political.

Peter Engelmann: Why did you decide to close the centre in 1984?

Jean-Luc Nancy: The question of civil society became a kind of *doxa*, but for Philippe and me it wasn't the fundamental problem we wanted to work on. I remember that Badiou suggested resuming the centre's work with a different angle. But then he went in his own political direction and I went to America in 1985, though I ended up only staying for two years.

Peter Engelmann: Where in America were you?

Jean-Luc Nancy: In San Diego. That was pure coincidence. I had met my present wife, Helene, and our son was born in 1985. Our problem was that Helene couldn't find a position in Strasbourg or in the vicinity, but we needed a second income. So I accepted a position in America at Jean-François's suggestion. But after two years it was clear to Helene and to me that we didn't want to stay in America. I'd been to Irvine for a week a number of times before that, but it's an entirely different experience to work at an American university – it's impossible – one's in a different world! At any rate, I continued to examine questions of community and the political after the centre closed. That same year, I was asked if

I wanted to put together an issue of *Cahiers de L'Herne* on Blanchot. I agreed and asked Philippe if he wanted to do it together with me. We started preparing the publication with Blanchot, we wanted to pursue the question of politics further. So we asked various people to contribute texts. After roughly two years it became clear that nobody wanted to write anything on that topic – except for academics doing PhDs on Blanchot, say. But we absolutely wanted to get some writers on board, people like Ungaretti or Enzensberger. Amazingly enough, they all turned us down with the argument that Blanchot was too important, that they couldn't write about him. Ultimately, we reached the conclusion that there were also political reasons for this: in 1982, a chapter from Jeffrey Mehlmann's book was published in *Tel Quel*, and there he examines Blanchot's proto-fascism and anti-Semitism in the 1930s. So Blanchot was also confronted with this accusation when he wrote *The Unavowable Community* – perhaps that was one reason why he didn't make his political stance entirely clear. So probably most of the people we had asked to contribute knew that the question of politics in Blanchot is very complicated, that the discussion about it might still continue, and that they would possibly risk arousing suspicion themselves. So we dropped the project.

Peter Engelmann: Was anything published about it later on?

Jean-Luc Nancy: No. Apparently there's a new project on Blanchot by L'Herne, but I don't know any details. It's very complicated, because there are still two warring factions when it comes to Blanchot. Anyway, I published a little book with Galilée in 2011, *Maurice Blanchot: Passion politique*.[24] This included a letter about Blanchot's political stance which he had written to us in the context of the planned edition of *Cahiers*. He didn't address it to Philippe or to me, however, but to Roger Laporte, a long-standing friend. At the end of the letter he wrote that Laporte could give the letter to Lacoue-Labarthe. This letter is very difficult to interpret. But engaging with the subject of community turned out to be increasingly difficult, not only in relation to Blanchot, because over time, people wanted to talk about it less and less, especially Jacques and Philippe – they didn't want to hear anything about community any more, albeit perhaps for very different reasons. Regarding Jacques: for a Francophone Jew, *communauté* also means the Jewish community (*la paroisse*), so it also has a religious meaning. You can imagine that he didn't want anything to do with that. True, he did go to synagogue in Nice on particular holidays with his sister, his brother, his father and mother, but he still had a very distant relationship with the Jewish community. Anyway, the word had a religious connotation for him. It was a different situation for Philippe, of course. But if he didn't reject community because of any religious associations, it was because of its affective, mystical baggage and its overtones of ethnic community.

Peter Engelmann: And this proximity doesn't bother you? Naturally it's problematic for a German.

Jean-Luc Nancy: Yes, I know that. When *The Inoperative Community* came out in German, a journalist at the *taz*[25] wrote, 'Nancy is a fascist!' Simply because I use the word 'community'. I didn't have these associations, but I'd never thought about it; it was only when Jean Christophe came up with the title *La communauté, le nombre* that this word became fully present-at-hand and ready-to-hand for me. It was only gradually that I too began to view the concept as problematic – though not so much for its connection to National Socialist ideology, but especially through the notion of inwardness evoked by community. What does this 'inside' mean? I understood that there was a contradiction in my use of this word. Because I was not talking precisely about inwardness, intimacy or things like that, but with the word 'community', I was operating in that exact semantic area. So, this made it necessary to think more closely about the issue of inwardness. Augustine said some important things about this. In the *Confessions* he says to God, 'But you were deeper inward to me than my most inward part and higher than my highest', which means that I can only refer to intimacy with myself if there is something that is even more inward than this intimacy. But what exactly does that mean? In the light of this, I subsequently began to speak more of *être-ensemble* [being-together] and *être-avec* [being-with], than of community. In *Being Singular Plural*[26] I spoke only of being-with. I even took the position that one should

64

rewrite *Being and Time*, taking Being-with, not mere Dasein, as the point of departure. That would require a specific existential analysis of the 'with' in Being-with. Nonetheless, I think that this 'with' – the Latin *cum*, as preserved in the French *communauté* – or also the *Gemein-* of *Gemeinschaft* doesn't necessarily, automatically have to end in some concept of inwardness. And that's what Heidegger means when he writes in §26 of *Being and Time* that the 'with' of Being-with should be understood existentially, not merely categorially. Unfortunately, he leaves it at this short note. This is how I read it: the categorial refers to the categories in Aristotle's sense, namely that with which one states something. In that sense, the 'with' would simply express a spatial and temporal coexistence. But 'with', which also invokes the centre [*Mitte*], means more than this: in Being-with, something becomes something, it is shared and conveyed, communicated – with brings us back to the Latin *cum*. In German one can also make the difference clear at the lexical level: one can use *neben* when speaking of the 'with' in the categorial sense, and save *mit* for the existential usage. That doesn't work in French, because we only have one word, *avec*, and that contains the Latin *apud*, which means 'in the vicinity of'. I've written about community on several occasions and in different ways, but I've never carried out a thorough analysis of this *mit* or *avec*. Maybe someone should do that. But I think one can say that the categorial 'with' as a mere 'alongside' may not actually exist, that as soon as something enters a relationship of 'alongside' with something else, an existential element also comes into play. We humans are never simply alongside one another; we always have something to do with one another as well, whether we want to or not. Sometimes it can seem as if this is not true, in everyday life in the street, for example. But something small, a minor accident, is enough to make it clear that people are not simply there alongside one another, but enter a relationship with one another. Or one takes the metro. Here is a man, there is a woman, and next to her a child. But one immediately notices various things: the man is old, the woman is dressed conspicuously and the child is holding a toy car. And if the train comes to a halt unexpectedly, people start talking to one another. 'Oh, is it going to take long?' and so on. And art knows this, it even makes it very obvious: if one puts different things alongside one another, for example in a still life, then something happens. The things aren't just there alongside one another, they enter a relationship; a context of meaning comes about, certainly not one with a concrete shape or autonomy, but there is a circulation between those elements.

Peter Engelmann: Between the 'alongsides'.

Jean-Luc Nancy: And that's the principle of every form of collection. If we look around the flat now, for example – these photos here, Picasso, the family at the dinner table, next to that a banknote … For the inhabitants, what looks like a mere juxtaposition has a sense.

Peter Engelmann: Something shared. Is that a shared sense?

Jean-Luc Nancy: Perhaps it's not so much a shared sense as a sense of shared life, a sense that can't necessarily be reduced to meaning.

Peter Engelmann: So you distinguish between sense and meaning?

Jean-Luc Nancy: Yes, the difference between sense and meaning is very important to me, though not in the same way that Frege, who wrote a famous essay about that, defines it. Meaning, *signification*, is something that takes place in language, the coming-together of the signifier and the signified.

Peter Engelmann: That's the differential theory of meaning as formulated by Saussure: the movement of the signifier and the signified creates meaning.

Jean-Luc Nancy: Yes. But sense, I would say, is far more than that. Sense comes about not only when we speak, but whenever some kind of communication takes place, when we look at one another, even when – as Heidegger says – we wave. We always, even involuntarily, give some indication of the mood we are in. What happens in this way I would call sense, rather than meaning. So, sense is first of all something that can be experienced sensually. Here, incidentally, one also sees the ambiguity of the word *Sinn* [sense] that was such a source of joy to Hegel, and lies in the fact that it refs both to the sensual and the spiritual. In addition, sense – as I understand it – is characterized by something that Bataille puts very well when he writes, *Il n'y a pas de sense pour un seul*: there is no sense for an individual. Here one can perhaps glimpse the possibility of a new beginning for philosophy, the possibility of not having to start from the individual. How could individuals exist if they were radically individual? They would neither be able to convey a sense nor would they have any sense themselves – they simply would not be in sense. And perhaps that means they wouldn't be at all. And that, I think, is the simplest way to prove that the one all-encompassing God is an impossibility. It is impossible to think a God alone, with no world, before the creation.

Peter Engelmann: So, God, like everything else, needs a counterpart, an other, in order to make sense?

Jean-Luc Nancy: Yes, yes. Sense always already means plurality. One must also interpret Leibniz's question against this background: why is there something rather than nothing? The problem is clearer in French, where one says, *Pourquoi y a-t-il quelque chose* – in the singular – *plutôt que rien?* But one should say *choses*, in the plural. So it's important to understand what Leibniz is talking about as a plurality. Because one thing on its own cannot exist. Hegel says that the One is its own destruction. Sense takes place only between several. There is always more than what is given. Perhaps one can say that giving itself is given, or the gift is given. And maybe the question, 'is a giver given here?' is a misleading question, since the giver would perhaps appear as singular. And for me this has an obvious connection to Hegel's foam that we were discussing, and also to Freud. In a letter to Marie Bonaparte, Freud writes about his dog. He writes that when his bitch plays in front of him, she seems utterly carefree and without a trouble in the world, and further on that anyone who starts asking questions about the sense in life is already a little ill. The mere question of sense is itself already an illness. Now, one mustn't think that being healthy consists in not having any relationship with sense. Being healthy rather means being fully within sense, immersing oneself in it and being subsumed by it, without asking questions, like Freud's bitch when she plays in front of her master. Freud then tells us that his bitch reminds him of Don Giovanni singing the Champagne Aria. Perhaps it's not entirely banal to ask, why champagne? Why sparkling wine, why prosecco? Why? – Because it foams! That is, because champagne is more than what is given with the champagne. It foams – perhaps a little bit longer, perhaps not: the fun is soon over. And with regard to art, one could show quite clearly, I think, that one is always dealing with a kind of excess. And that's exactly what people often say about the arts: that they're superfluous, excessive. But what does it mean if we need this excess? If excess is a necessity? I need a pencil to write, or perhaps to make a drawing. But why do I need excess, why champagne? Perhaps one will say, to get drunk! That would bring us to the subject of drunkenness, which is certainly a significant topic. In the history of philosophy there is one prominent example of a very peculiar drunkenness: why is it said of Socrates that he drank more than anyone else, yet without getting drunk? Drunk in the sense of dulled, mentally sluggish. It means, in my view, that he exposed himself to rapture more than anyone else, that he advanced into infinity, of which drunkenness can be one mode. Hegel later takes up this idea, for example, when he writes something in the preface to the *Phenomenology of Spirit* to the effect that truth is both the calm surface of still water and the drunken throng of Dionysus.

Peter Engelmann: Now if we try to look at the matter soberly again, then it's about looking for a 'more', for something that exceeds the given in the given. And you also want to counter politics as a mere administrative regime with this 'more'. You're looking for something that exceeds the limited sense of a politics understood in that way, for something that foams, for champagne. That's why you keep returning to Bataille, because that's also Bataille's theme, transgression. And, to connect this back to our themes, sense and community would be something transgressive, perhaps foaming, which is why it would be a mistake to envisage communication or politics by starting from the individual as the atom of meaning and society. Sense and community would be things that need to be thought not as a mere additive unity, but rather as proceeding from transgression?

Jean-Luc Nancy: Yes, absolutely. Especially with regard to politics, it seems to me that we've been defined – since its Greek beginnings – by the notion that practising it has to mean creating a unity.

IV

The Spirit of Communism

Peter Engelmann: Let's talk some more about how you distanced yourself from communism. Against the background of your deliberations so far, it seems to me that it wasn't really based on your experiences in 1968, but primarily on theoretical divergences.

Jean-Luc Nancy: The general idea at the time was simply to reform communism or Marxism, to adapt it to the different historical situation. But essentially people adhered to it, and the concern was only to make it more theoretically precise and potentially expand it. We, however, had different aims – though Marx always remained enormously important to me, of course. Today

I would even say that Marx understood that something is wrong deep inside our culture or civilization, not only in bourgeois society. Though he probably didn't know himself how thought could access that. Then his approach was to start from economy as something that structures society, and to see what insights can be gained from there. In one very famous passage, Marx says that religion is the spirit of a spiritless age.[27] I find that notable because it shows that spirit was somehow important to Marx. In retrospect, one can perhaps paraphrase this and say that the history of communism was a spiritless history. I don't mean to say that Lenin or Mao – I won't even speak of Stalin, as it seems to me that Stalin was no more than a common dictator – were spiritless people. But when Lenin says that communism is Soviet power plus the electrification of the whole country, I do ask myself if this illustrates the mistake made by communism when it allowed the scientific-rationalist overcoming of technological backwardness to replace spirit.

Peter Engelmann: You mean, Lenin mistakes what went by the name of 'spirit' in Marx for a technical-rationalist will to power?

Jean-Luc Nancy: I think that mistake can already be found in Marx's own work. Naturally, what I'm saying isn't meant to belittle his achievement. But perhaps we're better equipped today to see and to say that there's an element of Enlightenment thinking here, that his conception of rationality remains indebted to the Enlightenment – in that this privileging of economy as the ultimate authority indicates something over-rationalistic. Instead, one should locate the Marx who speaks of spirit. But what can spirit mean in his work? In my view: quite simply that God is dead. This not only means that Marx, like Nietzsche, is a critic of religion. Perhaps that's just an effect. The important thing is that he doesn't know what could replace God. After proclaiming the death of God, Nietzsche, as you know, lets the madman ask what sacred games will have to be invented to atone for his murder. But the question is left open. And perhaps what drove Nietzsche mad was that he recognized the problem very clearly, but had nothing with which to counter the condition of nihilism. By contrast, the Enlightenment thinker in Marx clings to the conviction that there's a rationality which could fill the gap left by God's death, a rationality that will produce a new spirit.

And this faith then becomes a faith in production, a faith that in production, he has found an object that secures the scientific nature of his insight, which is at once politically emancipatory. And in this production, he believes, people not only produce things, but also produce themselves as human beings. So Marx thinks this process in a similar way to Hegel's self-production of the spirit, albeit as material, technical production.

Peter Engelmann: But how is spirit supposed to come about through material production?

Jean-Luc Nancy: That's the question. I try to get to the bottom of what Marx is thinking when he says that religion is the spirit of a spiritless age. He must have had something in mind, he must have had some concept or notion of spirit. First of all, it means that religion is spiritless, it's the imitation of spirit, but is not itself spirit. My suspicion is that Marx takes spirit as the absolute value of the human being, or takes the human being as a value, which comes to the same thing.

Peter Engelmann: So then spirit would be the essence of the human being.

Jean-Luc Nancy: Yes, to the extent that the human being is the creature that produces itself. He writes somewhere that the spider weaves its web in a wondrous fashion, but differs from the architect – and this is the decisive point – because it doesn't have the structure in its head beforehand. That is, he sees the human being, in vary Kantian terms, as the only creature with the ability to turn the objects of its imagination into reality. That's essentially identical to Kant's definition of the will. Heidegger would object that when we speak of the will in this way, we remain trapped in the self-image of Western man as a force that produces the world from within itself as its own world. So the central aspect of the idea of production is not the question of whether it's a material or an ideational production, but rather the relationship between a subject, a project and its realization. So Marx probably sees spirit as the realization of the subject, and in this respect he remains faithful to Hegel.

Peter Engelmann: Do you see this, the metaphysical residue in Marx, as the real reason for the failure of communism?

Jean-Luc Nancy: The popular idea, as I said, was that Marxism was essentially the right way and simply had to be adapted to the new conditions. And we suspected at the time that this wasn't the right way to approach the problem. Because what if something was wrong with Marxism itself, if Marx himself was still trapped in the realm of metaphysics – in the sense of a metaphysics of presence and presence-at-hand, as discussed by Heidegger – after all? Heidegger's question of Being as a non-being influenced all of us – Derrida, Foucault, Deleuze – in different ways. Then we set about re-reading Marx, Nietzsche and also Husserl. And what transpired was that with them, in one way or another, Being is thought as a being. So what can it mean to think Being rigorously as a non-being? For me, that remains the central question of philosophy. And the question of spirit is exactly this question of Being as a non-being. If that is the case, one has to ask oneself what could have induced Heidegger to associate this spirit with Hitler? I say with Hitler, not with Nazism, because Heidegger knew that Nazism was a very crude metaphysics of beings – of race, blood and soil and so on. So, he believed in Hitler the man.

We know Heidegger's remark about the Fuhrer's beautiful hands. Beautiful hands – what can that mean but spirit? So, in a very strange way, there was a moment in which Hitler seemed to present spirit for Heidegger. And perhaps something similar went through Foucault's mind when he welcomed the Islamic Revolution as the return of the spiritual to politics.

Peter Engelmann: On the one hand, historical developments make it unlikely that a communist society can constitute the solution to all our problems; on the other hand, however, it's also the idea and the theory of communism – we spoke of Marx the Enlightenment thinker – that have become philosophically questionable, and especially questionable with regard to spirit. Can one still preserve the idea of communism at all?

Jean-Luc Nancy: Well, one can at least return to the core of this idea, the *communis* – the common, the communal.

Peter Engelmann: And that's the path your theoretical work took in 1968.

Jean-Luc Nancy: Yes. Fascism and actually existing communism made it obvious that the 'common' [*gemein*] inscribes its own particular ambiguity into community [*Gemeinschaft*] and every other word in which it appears, that is, both baseness [*Gemeinheit*] and a connection to the general [*das Allgemeine*]. This indicates both the possibility of a general sense and the will to a totalitarian form which does not open itself up to all, but rather puts itself in their place by forcing itself upon them.

Peter Engelmann: But isn't the positing of something general also – not only in the obvious case of positing as a totality, but also in the more discreet case of positing as the supposed offer of a general sense – the suppression and exclusion of particularities?

Jean-Luc Nancy: Yes, naturally there is a risk of privileging the general. But as I said earlier, reflections on community needn't necessarily lead to totalitarianism. Nonetheless, the concept does create a certain proximity to it. And that's the reason why some theorists – we already spoke of Derrida and Lacoue-Labarthe in this context – backed away from it. They saw the community as the general which is privileged over the individual. There were others who did use it: we've mentioned Blanchot, but Rancière also spoke of it and Agamben wrote *The Coming Community*.[28] Ultimately, one probably has to pose the question of the legitimacy of this opposition – the individual/the general – for oneself, for just as there is a totalitarianism that posits a general which suppresses the individual, there is also a totalitarianism of the individual. After all, what is the subject but the totality of an inwardness? In any case, I think that the word 'communism', in so far as community is contained in it, indicates the direction towards spirit – because community, meaning a connection to the other, is the thing in which sense or spirit comes about. We already said that sense is impossible for a single individual. From that perspective, communism wouldn't take the form of a government and the administration of the economy, but rather a shared sense in a joint life. We are always already together; in that sense, the community precedes the individual.

Peter Engelmann: And that's what an individual-based – atomistic – understanding of politics overlooks. This leads to the notion that the task of politics is to create a unity.

Jean-Luc Nancy: Yes. This understanding of politics goes back to Plato. Because the *Republic* was conceived and written with reference to a society that lacked unity; the unity displayed by each of the great theocratic empires had been lost. One can say that the polis is by its nature an attempt to restore the lost unity, and that Plato's *Republic* also constitutes a response to the question of how that might be possible.

Peter Engelmann: To the question of how one can create political unity in the situation of a society fragmented into individuals?

Jean-Luc Nancy: Yes. I think that the Greeks faced this challenge as a result of the destruction of the theocratic empires and the sacred order, whose framework probably hadn't even included anything like an individual yet. Probably the individual is even an effect of this collapse. Naturally there is good reason to say that the individual, in a pronounced sense, didn't exist yet in ancient Greece, and only came to fruition fully in Christianity. But the individual was already on the rise, so to speak.

Peter Engelmann: And you're saying that essentially, people always kept formulating the problem of politics within the coordinates of this specific historical situation?

Jean-Luc Nancy: Yes. The problem with that is that the French Revolution brought something into play that heightens and shifts this problematics in a radical way, because now the demand to get serious about democracy articulates itself. While Greek democracy was only open to a privileged group – the so-called freemen – and rested substantially on the exclusion of women, slaves and foreigners, the idea that all people are equal and equally free now takes root and starts to grow. That's something completely new. But to the same extent that this caesura can mean a liberation, it's also accompanied by a great responsibility and a considerable risk. Because the expansion of the democratic horizon also intensifies its heterogeneity. The plurality of individuals becomes a 'plurality of pluralities'. And suddenly one's confronted once again with the danger of a *belli omnium contra omnes* [war of all against all], which caused Hobbes so much worry and whose attempted prevention led to the totalitarianisms of the twentieth century.

Peter Engelmann: Would you say that both communism and fascism developed as reactions to this radical plurality?

Jean-Luc Nancy: I hold the view that they grew from the failure to give sense to plurality within the framework of democracy.

V

Democracy: Fixation or Circulation of Sense?

Peter Engelmann: We said that modern democracy differs substantially from Greek democracy, a democracy for freemen for which certain exclusions are constitutive.

Jean-Luc Nancy: Modern democracy marks a decisive cut: for the first time in the history of humanity, nothing is given to us any more. Greek democracy didn't have a problem with accepting certain things almost as given by nature – most of all slavery. There was no cause for discussion: whoever is captured in war becomes a slave. But for us, nothing is given in this way any more. And I think that because of that, politics is no longer given to us either, that politics as a toolbox of administrative means has had its day. I think this is something that Foucault sensed when he started becoming increasingly interested in different ways of ruling and being ruled. I don't know Foucault's work very well, but I suspect that when he said about the Iranian Revolution that the spiritual was entering politics again, he had something similar in mind. He soon backed away from that again. But maybe we haven't asked ourselves hard enough why he said that. After all, Foucault wasn't a Muslim, he wasn't a believer. I think he had a very acute awareness of the fact that politics – from that of the Greeks to that of the French Revolution – always needs to give itself a spiritual sense.

Peter Engelmann: A transcendental principle of legitimation?

Jean-Luc Nancy: Yes. That's the difference between the French and American revolutions. What matters isn't that the latter didn't present itself as a revolt to the same degree, but that the Declaration of Independence in which it culminated starts with God: God created humans in such a way that they have the right to act in an autonomous way. So, they received their autonomy from him; in that sense it's given to them.

Peter Engelmann: So, the French Revolution is a caesura, and then bourgeois society develops.

Jean-Luc Nancy: Bourgeois society is the society that recognizes no principle outside itself. The democratic republic is the legal-political unity of this society and guarantees its immanence. But bourgeois society is also the society of an incipient new mode of production: capitalism. Marx therefore held the view that democracy as a form of government is only the exterior of the real government, which consists in the play of economic forces. Badiou, who follows on from there, speaks of capitalo-parliamentarianism. As far as parliamentary, representative democracy is concerned, I share this assessment, without sharing his faith in a revolution. There's a close connection between democracy and capitalism. The development after the Second World War in particular makes it clear that democracy is the political form taken by the expansion of capitalism. This is where I see it as an intellectual trap always to think of democracy and totalitarianism in terms of oppositionality. Because to me, totalitarianisms stem from the failure of democracy to produce sense, and to be more than an administrative apparatus of capitalism.

Peter Engelmann: So, to summarize: ancient Greece saw the dissolution of the theocratic empires; the polis, perhaps Platonism itself, came about as a reaction to this collapse. As a result, our understanding of politics essentially remains shaped to this day by that historical moment in which politics sought to (re)establish a unity. Finally, with modern democracy, the explosive potential of this unity was intensified.

Jean-Luc Nancy: Yes. Perhaps we can put it like this: the inception of democracy was not only the beginning of a new form of politics, but of a new anthropology. Because democracy is not simply a procedure to establish a political unity or the form of this unity. Rather, the birth of democracy raised the question of whether the concern for political unity can justifiably constitute the only political concern. Naturally a minimum of homogeneity is required; we need laws, institutions and so forth. But the decisive question is whether the unity defined in this or that way enables the realization of sense. The self-conception of the historical social formations – classical democracy, the Roman Empire, feudalism, and the state of modernity as a state of sovereignty – started from the assumption that they would bring about the realization and circulation of sense. But there are grave doubts about that. It's likely that politics is always occupied with the formation of unity in one way or another, that it must seek to bring the multitude of individual interests and social forces into a certain organizational unity. But beyond this technical sense, we are still dealing with completely heterogeneous spheres of sense – thought, art and love, for example, so all the things that totalitarianism strives to deny.

Peter Engelmann: So, the democratic question is whether, against the background of a radically heterogeneous society, it is possible to avoid reducing the political to a striving for unity?

Jean-Luc Nancy: Yes, exactly. Democracy can't be content to produce a formal unity of society via technical procedures of administration; rather, it has to open up to what this unity cannot offer – that is, to all the different spheres of sense. And, against this background, one has to ask with every concrete political unity whether it opens up a space in which sense can realize itself and be circulated. The particularity of democracy also manifests itself in a different way. The word 'democracy' means: rule by the people. Very well. But what do we gain through it? Because one immediately has to ask who or what the people are. And we don't have a good answer to that. When we speak of theocracy, oligocracy, aristocracy and so on, we at least think we know what we're talking about. When we speak of democracy, on the other hand, we don't have a very specific idea. One can also see this in the fact that it's always a matter for debate at what age a person should be allowed to vote. When should one receive citizen status? In France, the voting age is eighteen; it used to be twenty-one. And it's possible that in the future, people will already be allowed to vote at sixteen. That means one doesn't know what a citizen is. Starkly put, one could say that in Athens and Rome and until the French Revolution, people knew more or less precisely what a free person was. There was clarity, to name a simple and powerful example, about whether a woman could be such a person too. And even during the French Revolution and at the beginning of the Republic, people were capable of deciding whether someone who didn't own any property and had to sell their labour power for a wage could also be a citizen. The answer – at least in lived practice – was no! Marx saw that very clearly: civil rights are the rights of citizens in the sense of the bourgeoisie, namely those who have property, and therefore they are chiefly proprietary rights. Democracy not only lets the people become owners of power, it also transforms them. The idea of the *demos* in democracy contains something that opens itself to the possibility of communication from the start. Democracy opens up for the people, for every person, the horizon of a shared provision of sense, but it doesn't fill it. In the previous social formations, by contrast, politics offered everyone not only a social order, but also a singular world of sense.

Peter Engelmann: So, the central point of politics concerned the belonging of humans to a world of sense, and the historical forms of society were different modalities of this belonging? Does that also apply to the nation state?

Jean-Luc Nancy: Yes! The nation is the idea that this belonging must be produced, if necessary by force. The French nation was created by the French kings and their ministers, sometimes very violently. In southern France they almost destroyed an entire civilization. In the sixteenth century, Francis I issued the edict of Villers-Cotterêts, which made French the sole administrative language. But long after that, many inhabitants of France still didn't speak the French language. In the time of Louis XIV, Madame de Maintenon founded a school in which children from the provincial aristocracy were to be taught French language and culture. There's a very good film about it. At the end of the film one sees a group of young daughters of nobles from the Bretagne, Languedoc, Alsace and so on, all speaking wildly at the same time in great excitement – but none of them are speaking French! And Madame de Maintenon says to them in French, 'Mademoiselles, you must become French!' The nation could only come about through the destruction of the entire feudal system. Think of Nicolas Fouquet, the last great feudal lord, who was thrown in prison by Louis XIV and whose property was annexed to the kingdom.

Peter Engelmann: So, the nation state offers a historical example of how, under the banner of an ideal – here the nation – social diversity was reduced. Then it remains the problem of democracy that it has to think universal equality and plurality together?

Jean-Luc Nancy: Yes, but in its efforts to do justice to plurality, it mustn't descend into a crude liberalism along the lines of 'Everyone does what they want'. Because, as everyone knows and everyone can see, this leads to a massive deficit of sense. The equality that arises in this way is actually an enormous inequality, because people don't all have the same chances or the same means to realize their supposed individual sense. Marx saw the ideological nature of this claim very clearly. The problem is that equality is reduced to mere equivalence, to equality before the law, for example, in such a way that the unlimited possibilities granted to each individual are simply formal possibilities, which not everyone has the same means to fill with content. If one proclaims, 'Everything for everyone!' it's vital to ask what this 'everything' is, and what kind of subject it is that one is so generously prepared to grant a share of it. In my opinion that's an important question. Let's take a look at the so-called democratization of school, for example. In France we have a situation today in which the democratization of schools has revealed itself for what it is: its genuine consequence is the reinforcement of the distance between the elites and everyone else. And it's clear to everyone that the French ministry of education currently has no interest in those who aren't destined for the elite. Naturally people often lament the low standard of education: 'The children can't speak or write well any more', and so forth. But in reality that's not a problem at all, because it's not necessary for everyone to be able to speak and write well. There's enough bad cinema and the like for those who remain untarnished by culture. One could easily get worked up because no one learns Greek any more. But what one would be neglecting to ask is whether there's actually any sense – and naturally

I don't just mean a financial sense, an economic use – for everyone to learn Greek. The ideology of democracy covers up this questionability by responding to this – and every other – political question by pointing to pure, universal equality. Then one says: everyone learns Greek. And then whoever doesn't make use of this supposed offer, which is actually a command, only has themselves to blame. Therefore the ideology of universal equality ultimately boils down to an apologia for the elites. That's the particular hypocrisy of democracy, or democratism. We think: yes, democracy – that's something everything for everyone. But that's a consumerist distortion of the actual situation. What do these words, 'everything' and 'everyone', mean here? One demands, 'Health for everyone!' But what does 'health' mean? How long should one be able or allowed to live? A hundred, two hundred years? Forever? This is an attitude that makes health subject to equivalence and to the logic of production. But what we don't know is how anything resembling sense is supposed to result from this.

Peter Engelmann: You're saying here that the idea of equality is reduced to the concept of equivalence. Let me play devil's advocate for a moment: wouldn't it at least be possible to ask whether the thinking of *différance*, that is, the semiotic turn in philosophy brought about by Derrida, among others, with his rejection of the representational model of language, in reality constitutes an assimilation of philosophy to capitalism? To the extent that capital floats and doesn't stay still in capitalism, meaning drifts in the universal text.

Jean-Luc Nancy: I don't think that's the case. The freedom of capital comes from equivalence in the exchange of commodities. When Derrida speaks of *différance* or Deleuze of difference, then I think this is always an appeal to a genuine difference, something other than the difference between a hundred and two hundred euros. Anthropologically put, it's about the difference of each person, about what Kant calls dignity (and whose status, by the way, strikes me as increasingly precarious).

Peter Engelmann: But doesn't this description substantialize difference? Can difference actually be anything? As a divergence, isn't it rather non-being or the non-determinable?

Jean-Luc Nancy: No, because *différance* with an 'a' isn't a divergence. It's the way – this is how I understand it, at least – in which a thing or the nature of a thing differs from itself, and is thus forced to becomes infinitely itself. That is, you become Peter Engelmann. But even when you die, you still won't have been Peter Engelmann completely. And yet somehow you will have been him. This 'have been' points to something that's simultaneously finished and unfinished, finite and infinite. Its meaning can't be fixed. So then it's not a matter of a substantialization – I'd even say: a subjectification – of difference, because an infinity opens up with every person or every living creature.

Peter Engelmann: Let's return to our central question, namely how one can give sense to democracy as community. Do you think the project of the European community is a possible answer to this question?

Jean-Luc Nancy: Historically there have certainly been different opportunities to refer to Europe as a shared sense. I'm thinking of the Europe of monasteries in the Middle Ages, the Europe of the Renaissance and the Enlightenment, or of the big cities, the bourgeoisie and trade in the nineteenth century. But then came a century of wars in which the nation state was at the centre as a unity that could provide sense, and destroyed any element of European sense that might have existed. So far, this fragmentation hasn't led to a new Europe, at least not one of sense. It's a popular question: will there be a united Europe again? I don't think it'll happen. Because, as I said, there's no shared form, no sense, that could unite Europe. Succinctly put: Europe has no sense, Europe has a market. A large market with many problems that finds it hard to become a real market, as it were, and Europe finds it even harder to become more than a market.

Peter Engelmann: So you're saying that the only narrative that works, because it supposedly provides sense, is the nation?

Jean-Luc Nancy: Yes. And that's why patriotism and national pride are flaring up everywhere today, and in some cases, like that of the *Lega Nord* in Italy, even regional pride. Perhaps Europe is a name that has been lent a different sense time and again over the centuries. One period in which Europe managed to give itself a shared sense was the Enlightenment: in the Enlightenment, people could feel like Europeans. From Voltaire to Goethe, from Hume to Frederick the Great … But the competition between the nation states began soon afterwards.

Peter Engelmann: But isn't it conceivable – and this is precisely what the post-war discourse is about – that one might overcome this competition, which cost millions of lives, within Europe in favour of commonality, not least recalling the 2,000 years of history in which there was a Europe, as you say? I wouldn't want to write off the project.

Jean-Luc Nancy: Today I would ask: isn't it already too late for that? Wasn't it already too late in 1945 too, when America and Russia divided up Europe among themselves and Europe found itself caught in the middle between a capitalism and what presented itself at the time as an anti-capitalism but, in reality, as we know today, was just a state capitalism – so that Europe was no more than the battleground on which one capitalism and another capitalism fought for supremacy?

Peter Engelmann: Well, in 1989 democratic capitalism won and expanded to European countries that previously belonged to the Soviet Union. Can't we entertain the hope that a new Europe might come about with the end of this division, or is everything already America anyway?

Jean-Luc Nancy: That's the question. I don't want to say whether I think that's the case. If I look out of the window here I see Paris, but if I go out into the street, if won't take long before I see McDonald's and so on.

Peter Engelmann: I don't think it's happened yet. I think that there's at least a longing for a European identity, a longing not to be America.

Jean-Luc Nancy: Yes, that's true. Perhaps it means that 'Europe' is becoming the term for the very thing we're talking about. A name for something for which we don't have a political model at the ready yet, which would also be the reason why we can't practise European politics. From that perspective, Europe would be the name for a sense that hasn't taken place yet, for a way of dealing with capitalism, technology, democracy and so forth that has yet to be defined, but which would be neither that of America nor of China.

Peter Engelmann: The attempt to enshrine the rule of law as a principle of society strikes me as characteristically European. In your opinion, would the expansion and consolidation of the rule of law be a worthwhile prospect?

Jean-Luc Nancy: That's a very difficult question. Let me just point out two things with reference to that: first of all, the rule of law is not a guarantee that prevents any severe violations of the law. Furthermore, the establishment of law always takes place via an exclusion. In the case of Europe, that might mean that its establishment would come at the cost of fencing it in.

Peter Engelmann: But that doesn't mean one should view the subject of the rule of law as finished. I had to encounter conditions in the GDR where the law didn't count, everything was controlled by the tyranny of the secret police and the central committees. Against this background, I think that the rule of law in Europe is very much worth striving for, both within the European states and in the relations between the states.

Jean-Luc Nancy: But you just said it yourself: within.

Peter Engelmann: But I also said, in the relations between the states.

Jean-Luc Nancy: But you're simply shifting the problem. One can see that in Schengen: we can't found a new Europe without establishing a new border around Europe.

Peter Engelmann: But how are things outside of Europe? We can see people fighting for the rule of law in Tunisia, for example, for regulated ways to negotiate between interests, the right to freedom of speech and similar things. Equal rights for women were recently enshrined in the constitution. Surely it would be arrogant to bury the question of human rights because we're so well off in Europe.

Jean-Luc Nancy: I agree with you, of course: we need human rights. But what we – perhaps only we philosophers – don't have to hand is the human. Who is the human of these human rights? We don't exactly know, even though we live in a world that began with Kant and his three questions of knowledge, morals and religion, which culminate in the fourth question, 'What is the human being?' We are a culture or a civilization that stands without the answer to its own question, as it were. Perhaps it's not such a bad thing to be without an answer, because it's possible that having an answer always leads to religion. Nonetheless, I don't think one should adopt a purely negative point of view. One can, for example, content oneself with only speaking of democracy in a negative way (as the absence of its own sense). Claude Lefort took this approach and spoke about democracy in a very American way, demanding that one should dispense with the symbolic presence of democracy in the same way one dispenses with a cult of personality. That's the topos of the jointly inhabited empty space of democracy, where no monument should be erected. That's already familiar from Jules Michelet – I think Lefort also quotes him – in whose time the Eiffel Tower hadn't been built yet and the Champ de Mars was still empty. In his history of the French Revolution, he writes: *Le Champ de Mars vide est le seul monument de la Republique* – the empty Champ de Mars is the only monument to the Republic, and the citizens can assemble in this empty space.[29] All right, but I always ask myself: is that enough? We're living in a different time now. The Champ de Mars has the Eiffel Tower, which in turn belongs to a time when technology could still monumentalize itself. The Eiffel Tower – that's technology sacralizing and monumentalizing itself. But the Eiffel Tower as a monument to technology is also the last of its kind. The most monumental thing in our time is probably the Internet, but that doesn't look like a monument. So, what have we gained, if we refrain from erecting a monument to democracy on the Champ de Mars or making reference to it in a positive fashion in our discourse? What does this shared place offer us, what kind of publicity is supposed to come about here? We don't know. That means the place that was supposed to be reserved for democracy remains empty. And to escape the quandary of this emptiness, we speak of elections. That's what leads to the constant repetitions of the same discussions about elections: what does it mean to vote? And one also hears the old slogan again: *élections, piège à cons* –

Peter Engelmann: A trap for fools.

Jean-Luc Nancy: Yes. A person who votes and believes they are carrying out a political act is really only performing an empty gesture. In 2012, the magazine *Ligne* devoted a whole issue to elections (I think I also wrote an essay for it). If you read that issue, you'll find that roughly half of the articles are in favour of elections, while the other half reject them. But even those in favour don't simply support elections; each one suggests different modalizations. In the light of this, Rancière suggested that one should go all the way with political equality and assign political posts, as the Greeks did for certain positions in the state, by *tirage au sort* – drawing lots.

Peter Engelmann: So that means that even elections can't give democracy any sense – they're simply a trap for fools. So, we remain in search of sense ...

Jean-Luc Nancy: I would say, yes, we're searching for spirit. The search for spirit, unlike the search for a better form of politics – to me, that's the decisive thing. Of course, it's probably possible here and there to improve politics in the technical sense, as administration. For example, you spoke in this context of expanding the rule of law. But the question remains, even in the face of such measures: what about spirit? Though one should also avoid speaking too hastily of spiritlessness. Perhaps spirit is indeed there, and one just has to know how to look. Perhaps it's the same as with God, of whom Hölderlin says that he's as evident as the sky.

Peter Engelmann: But you don't agree with that, do you?

Jean-Luc Nancy: Why not? I don't know. Naturally there are conditions that give one a strong urge to do something about them, for example to take steps to improve the lives of workers. And obviously that's desirable. But one shouldn't overlook the fact that the lives of the people one is seeking to help are not just limited to work and wages, or rather, that the work is part of a life praxis. There's now a direction in the theoretical study of work which is increasingly moving away from Marxism, because Marxism views work primarily in terms of wages and neglects the lives and the praxis of the workers.

Peter Engelmann: You're referring to the meaning of work for the workers?

Jean-Luc Nancy: Yes. Nowadays, with a company going bankrupt every other week and factories closing, one sees that very clearly. Because the workers who are losing their work and their wages as a result don't only lament the loss of what may be their only source of income, but also the loss of their activity. They're saying: we were the ones who produced this or that thing; we know how to make it and make it well; we prided ourselves in our work ...

Peter Engelmann: That means work has a sense for them – a spirit?

Jean-Luc Nancy: A spirit, yes. Naturally this spirit is very modest, very questionable, and if I speak of work in this way, it's certainly not unreasonable to accuse me, or at least to point to the danger, of secretly drifting rightwards and thus becoming a cryptoliberal who serenely claims that there are no problems with wage labour. Naturally that's not my intention. But I do think we've reached a point where it's no longer purely about working conditions and wage conditions. It's also about giving our coexistence a specific sense, and to ask where the spirit is in the face of this society, which wants to be neither one thing nor another and is therefore hardly a society at all. Until the nineteenth century, people knew in one way or another that sense can only come about in coexistence. Perhaps it's simply that we've forgotten that, and really don't know how to live with one another any more. But that's a drastic assessment that I can't entirely agree with. Because, as one can see, there is communication and we live together, even in a world of globalization that enables us in a completely different way to engage with foreign languages, customs and cultures. The forms of Asian or African art, for example, are no longer as foreign to us as they were for Europeans in the eighteenth century.

Peter Engelmann: You say, with certain qualifications, that community – or at least the knowledge about community – has been lost. I would disagree. I think that even after the emergence of the nation state as a political principle, communities didn't disappear. There are still national communities, communities of faith or interests, and so on. And people also see themselves as communal beings, as part of one community or another.

Jean-Luc Nancy: Naturally people still nominally belong to communities today: they're members in communities of work or interests. But if one looks for a moment at the national communities you refer to: where do national communities stand today, what significance does the nation have for the community? What does the popularity of regional autonomy movements in Europe mean in this context, for example?

Peter Engelmann: Do you mean to say that the sense of these types of community is somewhat lacking, especially because of their particularism? There's never been a global or universal community.

Jean-Luc Nancy: No, the problem lies elsewhere. Communities call each other into question because there are competing senses of belonging. For humans, that leads to the problem of their identity. One asks oneself: am I an Arab or a Muslim; can one be an Arab without being a Muslim? Am I first of all a Frenchman or a Catholic? That plays an important part in the current debate in France about same-sex marriage, for example. Fundamentally speaking, one can say that Europe is defining itself less and less as a community of faith. That's quite different in America, where the motto is still 'God bless America'. On the one hand, many people who used to define themselves as Christians have become humanists, socialists and so forth. That's more or less true of me. On the other hand, Islam has a stronger presence in Europe than before, and brings into play its very own understanding of the relationship between humans and God or the community.

Peter Engelmann: So, there are various attempts to find and provide sense among highly particularized communities, each with their own horizon of sense.

Jean-Luc Nancy: The field of the political has always been characterized by a certain ambiguity: on the one hand, people simply expect politics to regulate social forces and interests, but on the other hand, politics should also be the name for precisely what we've called community, for a sense or spirit. But naturally there's a suspicion that from Rome to the Third Reich, this spirit, in its various manifestations, was never anything but an idol – an empty, spiritless phantasm for the benefit of those in power and to the detriment of all others. Yet one can also ask oneself whether Bataille, when he wrote about the *gloire du roi* – the glory of the king – which radiated positively upon all his subjects, was pointing to something true. Bataille himself doesn't insist on it, and concludes that the whole of history is rather a sad history of oppression and war. But to me, the question remains nonetheless.

Peter Engelmann: You're saying that those weren't just idols, there was genuine spirit there?

Jean-Luc Nancy: I'm saying that it remains an open question. Was Marx right – and others too,

Nietzsche and Kierkegaard – when he declared his time a spiritless one?

Peter Engelmann: That was the usual diagnosis from the middle of the nineteenth century on.

Jean-Luc Nancy: Yes. But Heidegger took it a step further when he said, in his famous interview with *Der Spiegel*, that even democracy can't save us, only a new god can. What does that mean? Some people drew the most obvious conclusion and spoke of Heidegger's turn towards religion. But I don't think it's as simple as that. Heidegger was more intelligent than that. The mention of God can only be a reference to the possibility of a sense being somehow conveyed in society. It's along the same lines as Pascal's dictum that man infinitely surpasses man. The question of spirit is the question as to the possibility of humans to gain access to something superhuman.

Peter Engelmann: And religion offers a possible way to achieve that?

Jean-Luc Nancy: Yes, but religion, as far as we know, was also always a means of social oppression.

Peter Engelmann: That means that religion presents us with the same situation as communism: both of them are characterized by the ambiguity that on the one hand, they aim to provide sense, yet on the other hand – as far as their historical realizations go – they lead to oppression and death.

Jean-Luc Nancy: Perhaps it was even worse with communism than with the church. What's clear is that the old ways of asking and answering won't get us any further. We have to understand that we're at the start of a new era, where it leads nowhere to keep bringing the same means and ends into play. It's a matter of developing a feeling, a notion of what new things are in the process of emerging. That's very difficult, of course. At the beginning we spoke about how I had the feeling with Derrida back then that something new, a new way of philosophizing was in the offing. Derrida wasn't alone; Deleuze, Foucault and others had a share in it too. Of course, everything isn't renewed at the same time, there are regressions and the like. We saw how in Marx, for example, there is already an ambivalence: the adherence to the rationality of the Enlightenment and the thematization of spirit. I hold the view that this intuition also manifests itself in the work of other philosophers. I'm thinking of Nietzsche's eternal recurrence, Kierkegaard's relation to the absolute, and of course Heidegger's *Ereignis*. If one takes a look at the history of art, one will likewise find intimations of something new here. Think of Cézanne, who, in the nineteenth century, began painting in a way that perhaps wasn't just unusual at the time, but even – against the background of established art – could be interpreted as a mistake, an error of painting. In music, it was above all Wagner who paved the way for a transformation of music with his endless melody.

Editor's Afterword

The most important advance in philosophical knowledge during the last third of the twentieth century was Jacques Derrida's development of the philosophy of difference via the critique of metaphysics. Derrida's deconstruction of logocentrism as phonocentrism, and its unmasking as the ground of metaphysics, revolutionized Western philosophy. His discovery of the productivity of writing as an authorless, non-phonocentric, non-logocentric, non-metaphysical possibility of constituting meaning not only opened up the possibility of new readings of our texts, but also a new understanding of creativity and renewal in the various areas of human action. The deconstructive gaze uncovers foundations, grounds, authorities, securities and certainties as constructs. In doing so, however, it also shows us the possibility of other constructs that are no less legitimate than the old, deconstructed ones.

The strength of these constructs, which emerged from deconstruction, is that they cannot be absolutized without revealing their origins in a deconstructive act. Therefore, they offer a certain protection against absolutizations, and thus against political totalitarianism, as Jacques Derrida argued in one of his relatively rare political writings. In the field of the political and for our psyche, this strength is at once a weakness. Because deconstruction relativizes everything absolute, or purportedly absolute, and sets it in motion, it takes away the security of an absolute certainty and thus makes us afraid. When one leaves the realm of philosophy, literature and the arts, one is immediately confronted with totalitarian demands that cannot be relativized, and which the deconstructive mode of thinking cannot counter with absolutizations without calling its own approach into question and betraying its basic intention.

Although Derrida expounded the political relevance of deconstruction in the Paul de Man affair, there is still no concept of a deconstructive politics with any prospect of establishing itself in the political space. Rather, every encounter with the sphere of politics seems to endanger the reserved approach of difference-philosophical thought. Thus, it is surely a lacuna in the deconstructive method that most authors associated with it concentrated on dismantling identities, but then failed to put together what they had taken apart. In this way, the deconstructive paradigm took on the appearance of an esoteric and clearly unworldly mode of thought.

We can understand this one-sidedness if we think of how aggressively and vehemently Derrida's thought, and the philosophies that followed on from it, were attacked. Because it was so new and untested, it first required the presentation of studies that would reinforce and defend it before it could proceed further. Today we have hopefully reached a point where we can explore the constructive possibilities of deconstruction more courageously.

In my view, the most important author for this further development of deconstruction is my conversational partner in the present book, Jean-Luc Nancy, whose efforts to develop this constructive, socially, culturally and politically relevant side of difference-philosophical thought already began in the 1980s. For some time, the concept of community, heavily burdened by its frequent totalitarian application, has been the main focus of his reflections. Nancy attempts to free this concept from its totalitarian overdetermination, and to rethink it in the deconstructive tradition in such a way that it can become available to us and serve as a starting point for new reflections on democracy.

The concept of democracy is also highly fraught after the social crises resulting from the crisis in the financial industry. After all, democracy is the social form which not only failed to prevent the excesses of financial capitalism but, on the contrary, created the political conditions for it to function in the first place. Without the material and ideological structures, the power apparatuses and dumbing-down industries of our democracy, this development would not have been possible without enormous resistance.

I do not consider totalitarian armament with historically refuted concepts, as found in the work of such thinkers as Alain Badiou and Slavoj Žižek, an alternative to this. The reflections of Colin Crouch on a new equilibrium between the market and politics can probably be functionally integrated too easily, without effecting any fundamental change. But we need reflections that attempt to lead us out of the present cul-de-sac of our economic and social order. That is why Jean-Luc Nancy's approach of thinking the concept of a radical democracy from a community that is neither posited absolutely nor distorted in totalitarian fashion is so important for our time. His philosophical reflections, like those of Alain Badiou, Slavoj Žižek or Colin Crouch, are of great social relevance.

The obscene socialization of private losses through the financial industry calls into question the legitimacy of our social organization and our political system, which was caught completely unawares by such lootings, which were evidently able to develop unhindered in a system-immanent fashion. Hence the question of political legitimacy and social order today is not a matter of social minorities and marginalized groups, but rather a question from the centre of our society: what can we use to combat the destruction of our social order and our political system of Western democracy, this destruction of our society from within?

In this volume of conversations, I have attempted to explore with Jean-Luc Nancy the possibilities for a new social legitimacy, proceeding from his category of community and his reflections on a radical democracy.

The conversation with Jean-Luc Nancy took place in Paris during two days in May 2014.

This book is the result of a joint effort. In addition to Jean-Luc Nancy, I would like to thank Alexandra Reininghaus for accompanying these conversations, and Boris Kränzel and Eva Luise Kühn for the difficult work of editing and proofreading the material.

Peter Engelmann

Notes

1 An English translation of this pamphlet, which was published by the situationists in 1966 in a batch of 10,000 copies at the expense of the University of Strasbourg, can be found online at https://archive.org/details/OnThePovertyOfStudentLife

2 'The Glorious Thirty', referring to the period from 1945–1975 (trans.).

3 Jacques Derrida, *Voice and Phenomenon: Introduction to the Problem of the Sign in Husserl's Phenomenology*, trans. Leonard Lawlor (Evanston: Northwestern University Press, 2011).

4 Jacques Derrida, *Of Grammatology*, trans. Gayatri Chakravorty Spivak (Baltimore: Johns Hopkins University Press, 1997).

5 G. W. F. Hegel, *Phenomenology of Spirit*, trans.

A. V. Miller (Oxford and New York: Oxford University Press, 1977).

6 Ibid., p. 493.

7 Martin Heidegger, 'Letter on Humanism', trans. Frank A Capuzzi, in *Pathmarks*, ed. William McNeil (Cambridge: Cambridge University Press, 1998), pp. 239–76.

8 Jean-Paul Sartre, *Existentialism Is a Humanism*, ed. John Kulka, trans. Carol Macomber (New Haven: Yale University Press, 2007). Despite the title of the published English version, the original title translates as 'Is Existentialism a Humanism?' (trans.).

9 Martin Heidegger, *Being and Time*, trans. John Macquarrie and Edward Robinson (Oxford: Blackwell, 1978).

10 Martin Heidegger, 'Anaximander's Saying', in *Off the Beaten Track*, ed. and trans. Julian Young and Kenneth Haynes (Cambridge: Cambridge University Press, 2002), pp. 242–79.

11 On the concept of *destinerrance*, see Jacques Derrida, 'Let Us Not Forget – Psychoanalysis', trans. Geoffrey Bennington and Rachel Bowlby, in *Psychoanalysis and Literature: New Work*, ed. Nicholas Royle and Ann Wordsworth, *Oxford Literary Review* 12 (1990): 3–7.

12 Sigmund Freud, *Moses and Monotheism: Three*

Essays, in *The Standard Edition of the Complete Works of Sigmund Freud*, ed. James Strachey et al. (London: The Hogarth Press / The Institute of Psychoanalysis, 1953–1974), vol. 23 (1964).

13 Giacomo Todeschini, *Franciscan Wealth: From Voluntary Poverty to Market Society*, trans. Donatella Melucci, ed. Michael F. Cusato O.F.M., Jean François Godet-Calogeras and Daria Mitchell O.S.F. (New York: Franciscan Institute, 2009).

14 Jacques Derrida, 'White Mythology: Metaphor in the Text of Philosophy', in *Margins of Philosophy*, trans. Alan Bass (Chicago: University of Chicago Press, 1982), pp. 207–27.

15 Philippe Lacoue-Labarthe and Jean-Luc Nancy, *The Literary Absolute: The Theory of Literature in German Romanticism*, trans. Philip Barnard and Cheryl Lester (New York: SUNY Press, 1988).

16 Philippe Lacoue-Labarthe and Jean-Luc Nancy, 'La panique politique', trans. Céline Surprenant, in *Retreating the Political*, ed. Simon Sparks (London and New York: Routledge, 2005), pp. 1–31.

17 Philippe Lacoue-Labarthe and Jean-Luc Nancy, 'The Jewish People Do Not Dream', trans. Brian Holmes, in *Stanford Literature Review* 6, no. 2 (1989): 191–209.

18 Philippe Lacoue-Labarthe and Jean-Luc Nancy, 'The Nazi Myth', trans. Brian Holmes, in *Critical Inquiry* 16 (Winter 1990): 291–312.

19 Jean-Luc Nancy, *The Inoperative Community*, ed. Peter Connor, trans. Peter Connor, Lisa Garbus, Michael Holland and Simona Sawhney (Minneapolis and London: Minnesota University Press, 1991).

20 Maurice Blanchot, *The Unavowable Community*, trans. Pierre Joris (Barrytown: Station Hill Press, 1991).

21 Marguerite Duras, *The Malady of Death*, trans. Barbara Bray (New York: Grove Press, 1986).

22 Maurice Blanchot, *Les Intellectuels en question. Ébauche d'une réflexion* (Paris: Fourbis, 1996).

23 Jacques Derrida, *Politics of Friendship*, trans. George Collins (London: Verso, 1997).

24 Jean-Luc Nancy, *Maurice Blanchot: Passion politique* (Paris: Galilée, 2011).

25 A German daily newspaper; the name is abbreviated from *Die Tageszeitung* [The Daily Newspaper] (trans.).

26 Jean-Luc Nancy, *Being Singular Plural*, trans. Anne O'Byrne and Robert Richardson (Stanford: Stanford University Press, 1999).

27 The original passage reads as follows: 'Religion is the sigh of the oppressed creature, the heart

of a heartless world and the spirit of spiritless conditions.' From Karl Marx, *Critique of Hegel's 'Philosophy of Right'*, ed. Joseph O'Malley, trans. Annette Jolin and Joseph O'Malley (Cambridge: Cambridge University Press, 1970) (translation modified).

28 Giorgio Agamben, *The Coming Community*, trans. Michael Hardt (Minneapolis: University of Minnesota Press, 1993).

29 Jules Michelet, *History of the French Revolution* (1847), trans. Charles Cocks (Whitefish, MT: Kessinger, 2010).